THE
PATRIOT
ACT

Opposing Viewpoints®

THE
PATRIOT
ACT

Opposing Viewpoints®

Other Books of Related Interest

THE PATRIOT ACT

Opposing Viewpoints®

Louise I. Gerdes, *Book Editor*

Bruce Glassman, *Vice President*
Bonnie Szumski, *Publisher*
Helen Cothran, *Managing Editor*

OPPOSING
VIEWPOINTS®
SERIES

GREENHAVEN PRESS
An imprint of Thomson Gale, a part of The Thomson Corporation

THOMSON
™
GALE

Detroit • New York • San Francisco • San Diego • New Haven, Conn.
Waterville, Maine • London • Munich

THOMSON

GALE

LIBRARY OF CONGRESS CATALOGING-IN-PUBLICATION DATA

The Patriot Act : opposing viewpoints / Louise I. Gerdes, book editor.
   p. cm. — (Opposing viewpoints series)
   Includes bibliographical references and index.
   ISBN 0-7377-3097-8 (lib. : alk. paper) — ISBN 0-7377-3098-6 (pbk. : alk. paper)
   1. United States. Uniting and Strengthening America by Providing
Appropriate Tools Required to Intercept and Obstruct Terrorism (USA PATRIOT
ACT) Act of 2001. 2. Civil rights—United States. 3. Terrorism—United
States—Prevention. 4. National security—Law and legislation—United States.
I. Gerdes, Louise I., 1953– . II. Opposing viewpoints series (Unnumbered)
KF9430.P38 2005
345.73'02—dc22   2004060591

Printed in the United States of America

"Congress shall make
no law...abridging the
freedom of speech, or of
the press."

First Amendment to the U.S. Constitution

The basic foundation of our democracy is the First
Amendment guarantee of freedom of expression.
The Opposing Viewpoints Series is dedicated to the
concept of this basic freedom and the idea that it is
more important to practice it than to enshrine it.

Contents

Why Consider Opposing Viewpoints?

"The only way in which a human being can make some approach to knowing the whole of a subject is by hearing what can be said about it by persons of every variety of opinion and studying all modes in which it can be looked at by every character of mind. No wise man ever acquired his wisdom in any mode but this."

John Stuart Mill

In our media-intensive culture it is not difficult to find differing opinions. Thousands of newspapers and magazines and dozens of radio and television talk shows resound with differing points of view. The difficulty lies in deciding which opinion to agree with and which "experts" seem the most credible. The more inundated we become with differing opinions and claims, the more essential it is to hone critical reading and thinking skills to evaluate these ideas. Opposing Viewpoints books address this problem directly by presenting stimulating debates that can be used to enhance and teach these skills. The varied opinions contained in each book examine many different aspects of a single issue. While examining these conveniently edited opposing views, readers can develop critical thinking skills such as the ability to compare and contrast authors' credibility, facts, argumentation styles, use of persuasive techniques, and other stylistic tools. In short, the Opposing Viewpoints Series is an ideal way to attain the higher-level thinking and reading skills so essential in a culture of diverse and contradictory opinions.

In addition to providing a tool for critical thinking, Opposing Viewpoints books challenge readers to question their own strongly held opinions and assumptions. Most people form their opinions on the basis of upbringing, peer pressure, and personal, cultural, or professional bias. By reading carefully balanced opposing views, readers must directly confront new ideas as well as the opinions of those with whom they disagree. This is not to simplistically argue that everyone who reads opposing views will—or should—change his or her opinion. Instead, the series enhances readers' understanding of their own views by encouraging confrontation with opposing ideas. Careful examination of others' views can lead to the readers' understanding of the logical inconsistencies in their own opinions, perspective on why they hold an opinion, and the consideration of the possibility that their opinion requires further evaluation.

Evaluating Other Opinions

To ensure that this type of examination occurs, Opposing Viewpoints books present all types of opinions. Prominent spokespeople on different sides of each issue as well as well-known professionals from many disciplines challenge the reader. An additional goal of the series is to provide a forum for other, less known, or even unpopular viewpoints. The opinion of an ordinary person who has had to make the decision to cut off life support from a terminally ill relative, for example, may be just as valuable and provide just as much insight as a medical ethicist's professional opinion. The editors have two additional purposes in including these less known views. One, the editors encourage readers to respect others' opinions—even when not enhanced by professional credibility. It is only by reading or listening to and objectively evaluating others' ideas that one can determine whether they are worthy of consideration. Two, the inclusion of such viewpoints encourages the important critical thinking skill of objectively evaluating an author's credentials and bias. This evaluation will illuminate an author's reasons for taking a particular stance on an issue and will aid in readers' evaluation of the author's ideas.

It is our hope that these books will give readers a deeper understanding of the issues debated and an appreciation of the complexity of even seemingly simple issues when good and honest people disagree. This awareness is particularly important in a democratic society such as ours in which people enter into public debate to determine the common good. Those with whom one disagrees should not be regarded as enemies but rather as people whose views deserve careful examination and may shed light on one's own.

Thomas Jefferson once said that "difference of opinion leads to inquiry, and inquiry to truth." Jefferson, a broadly educated man, argued that "if a nation expects to be ignorant and free . . . it expects what never was and never will be." As individuals and as a nation, it is imperative that we consider the opinions of others and examine them with skill and discernment. The Opposing Viewpoints Series is intended to help readers achieve this goal.

David L. Bender and Bruno Leone,
Founders

Greenhaven Press anthologies primarily consist of previously published material taken from a variety of sources, including periodicals, books, scholarly journals, newspapers, government documents, and position papers from private and public organizations. These original sources are often edited for length and to ensure their accessibility for a young adult audience. The anthology editors also change the original titles of these works in order to clearly present the main thesis of each viewpoint and to explicitly indicate the opinion presented in the viewpoint. These alterations are made in consideration of both the reading and comprehension levels of a young adult audience. Every effort is made to ensure that Greenhaven Press accurately reflects the original intent of the authors included in this anthology.

Introduction

"By expanding the nature of the information that can be captured, the [Patriot Act] clearly expanded pen register capacities to the Internet, covering electronic mail, Web surfing, and all other forms of electronic communications. The full impact of this expansion of coverage is difficult to assess."

—Electronic Privacy Information Center

One week after the September 11, 2001, terrorist attacks, the Bush administration submitted a legislative proposal to combat terrorism called the Uniting and Strengthening America by Providing Appropriate Tools Required to Intercept and Obstruct Terrorism Act of 2001 (Patriot Act). The Patriot Act passed in the Senate without debate. After minor changes were made in the House, the complex, 342-page bill passed 357 to 66 and was signed into law on October 26, 2001.

Since that time, controversy over the Patriot Act has been heated. The debate centers around two competing interests: enhancing national security and protecting civil liberties. According to the Department of Justice (DOJ), "The USA PATRIOT Act equips federal law enforcement and intelligence officials with the tools they need to mount an effective, coordinated campaign against our nation's terrorist enemies." The American Civil Liberties Union (ACLU) claims, on the other hand, that the Patriot Act "vastly expand[s] the government's authority to spy on its own citizens, while simultaneously reducing checks and balances on those powers like judicial oversight, public accountability, and the ability to challenge government searches in court." The debate over the Patriot Act's impact on Internet activities reflects these competing views.

Before the Patriot Act, Internet surveillance was unregulated. Whether a judge would authorize Internet surveillance depended on the judge's decision to apply "pen register" and "trap-and-trace" laws to Internet communications. Pen register surveillance devices capture the phone numbers dialed on outgoing telephone calls; trap-and-trace devices capture the numbers identifying incoming calls. Because investigators hoping to gain approval to use these devices were not required to prove probable cause that a crime was being committed, the courts traditionally limited surveillance to obtaining telephone numbers alone and prohibited law enforcement from obtaining the content of telephone calls. Despite those limitations, this type of surveillance can be quite useful. According to the Center for Democracy & Technology, "In an increasingly connected world, a recording of every telephone number dialed and the source of every call received can provide a very complete picture—a profile—of a person's associations, habits, contacts, interests and activities. For that reason, pen registers and trap and trace devices are very helpful to law enforcement." Hoping to gain similar information from Internet communications, law enforcement pursued surveillance warrants for Internet addresses, also known as URLs. While some judges applied the surveillance law to Internet surveillance, others did not.

The Patriot Act closes the gap between telephone and Internet surveillance law. Section 216 grants federal agents the authority to apply pen register and trap-and-trace law to the Internet. Judges may now grant surveillance warrants to obtain the Internet addresses that a suspect visits. The Patriot Act also expands the circumstances under which law enforcement may obtain these warrants, which were defined by the 1978 Foreign Intelligence Surveillance Act. FISA provided an exception to the Fourth Amendment requirement that surveillance warrants require a showing of probable cause. The purpose of the exception was to allow law enforcement to gather foreign intelligence; federal agencies would not be able to use surveillance warrants as a means to spy on Americans. To obtain a FISA surveillance warrant, law enforcement had to prove that the surveillance target was "an agent of a foreign power." Section 214 of the Patriot Act expands the use of surveillance warrants to reveal information "relevant to investigations intended to protect against international terrorism or 'clandestine intelligence activities.'" The DOJ claims that Section 216 has made it easier to track the communications of terrorists, making ap-

15

prehension easier; it also contends that Section 214 has been used to investigate suspected terrorist operatives.

Civil liberties proponents are not comforted by claims that the Patriot Act thwarts terrorists. They argue that secret surveillance warrants granted without probable cause constitute a violation of privacy. These critics approved of the pre–Patriot Act law governing pen register and trap-and-trace surveillance warrants because phone numbers do not contain content and most Americans do not expect their phone numbers to be private. Unlike telephone numbers, however, Web addresses and e-mail contain content, and people expect their Internet content to remain private, advocates of civil liberties point out. The ACLU maintains,

> The URLs or "addresses" of the Web pages we read are not really addresses, they are the titles of documents that we download from the Internet. When we "visit" a Web page what we are really doing is downloading that page from the Internet onto our computer. . . . That is much richer information than a simple list of the people we have communicated with; it is intimate information that reveals who we are and what we are thinking about—much more like the content of a phone call than the number dialed.

In addition, civil libertarians claim that Section 214 of the Patriot Act allows law enforcement to spy on American citizens who use the Internet. While FISA required a showing that the surveillance target was "an agent of a foreign power," Section 214 only requires that the information be relevant to terrorist investigations, requiring no showing that the Internet user is a foreign agent. The Electronic Privacy Information Center argues,

> [Section 214 of the Patriot Act] significantly eviscerates the consitutional rationale for the relatively lax requirements that apply to foreign intelligence surveillance. The laxity is premised on the assumption that the Executive Branch, in pursuit of its national security responsibilities to monitor the activities of foreign powers and their agents, should not be unduly restrained by Congress and the courts. The removal of the "foreign power" predicate for pen register/trap and trace surveillance upsets that delicate balance.

Whether the Patriot Act effectively balances the need to enhance national security and protect the civil liberties of

Internet users remains controversial. The authors in *Opposing Viewpoints: The Patriot Act* express their views on this and other questions in the following chapters: Does the Patriot Act Enhance National Security? Does the Patriot Act Violate Civil Liberties? Should the Patriot Act Be Amended? How Have Americans Reacted to the Patriot Act? As the debate over Patriot Act provisions concerning Internet surveillance makes clear, maintaining the balance between privacy and security is extraordinarily difficult.

CHAPTER 1

Does the Patriot Act Enhance National Security?

Chapter Preface

Six weeks after the terrorist attacks of September 11, 2001, Congress passed the 342-page Patriot Act without the deliberation and debate typical of the passing of most legislation.

Just eight days after the attacks, during a period of intense national unity and support for the government, the Bush administration, experiencing an approval rating of 90 percent, submitted the Patriot Act to Congress, claiming it would give federal law enforcement the tools it needed to fight terrorism. According to the Center for National Security Studies, "The attorney general demanded that Congress pass the bill within a week and without change." Nevertheless, chairman of the Senate Judiciary Committee, Patrick Leahy, won some changes in negotiations with the Justice Department. At the same time in the House, Congressmen Jim Sensenbrenner and John Conyers began similar negotiations that some claim led to substantial improvements in the bill.

However, the Bush administration and Attorney General John Ashcroft continued to pressure Congress to pass the bill, warning that additional terrorist acts were imminent. According to the American Civil Liberties Union, "The Bush Administration implied that members who voted against it would be blamed for any further attacks—a powerful threat at a time when the nation was expecting a second attack to come any moment." An all-night negotiation among Senate leaders led to a bipartisan bill that took back most of Senator Leahy's changes, and this proposal passed without debate or amendment. Only Senator Russell Feingold voted against the bill. The House also sacrificed the changes it had made in its all-night drafting session. The House bill was rushed to the floor and passed with only three Republican and seventy-five Democratic votes in opposition.

While many commentators argue that the rush to pass the Patriot Act has left America with a poor piece of legislation, others assert that it was necessary to speed up the legislative process to protect the nation against terrorists. In times of national emergency, Americans look to their government to act, and to act quickly. The authors in the following chapter examine to what extent the Patriot Act lives up to its goal of enhancing national security.

| "The tools of the Patriot Act are vital to our ability to prevent terrorist attacks."

The Patriot Act Enhances National Security

Tom Ridge

The information-sharing and investigative tools granted to law enforcement by the Patriot Act protect national security by disrupting terrorist plots against the United States, argues Director of Homeland Security Tom Ridge in the following viewpoint. Before the terrorist attacks of September 11, 2001, U.S. foreign intelligence agencies and criminal investigative agencies such as the FBI could not share information vital to fighting terrorism, Ridge maintains. Since the implementation of the information-sharing provisions of the act, he contends, several terrorists have been successfully convicted. The act's investigative tools have also foiled terrorist plots, Ridge claims. This viewpoint was originally given as a speech at the Allegheny County Emergency Operations Center in Pennsylvania on July 15, 2004.

As you read, consider the following questions:
1. According to Ridge, how had law enforcement used the investigative tools of the Patriot Act before it was enacted?
2. What is required to accomplish the ultimate goal of preventing terrorist attacks, in the author's view?
3. In the author's opinion, what kind of strategy is necessary to successfully protect the United States from those who wish to do it harm?

Tom Ridge, address at the Allegheny County Emergency Operations Center, July 15, 2004.

Today I am here to talk about the Patriot Act—and how its core tools are essential to the success of the single most important mission of the Department of Homeland Security [DHS]—to prevent another terrorist attack from happening in the United States.

I've said it many times. We share nearly 7,500 miles of land border with Canada and Mexico, across which more than 400 million people, 130 million motor vehicles, and 2.5 million rail cars pass every year.

We patrol almost 95,000 miles of shoreline and navigable waters, and 361 ports that see 8,000 foreign flag vessels, 9 million containers of cargo, and nearly 200 million cruise and ferry passengers every year. We have to get it right millions of times a week.

But the terrorists only have to get it right once.

The Tools to Prevent Terrorism

Under President [George W.] Bush's leadership, the Department of Homeland Security now has many new tools at its disposal to help us "get it right". Today, I want to talk about one of these new tools: the USA Patriot Act. The Patriot Act includes two of the most powerful mechanisms available to America today to prevent future attacks.

One is the potent new information sharing provisions contained in the Patriot Act. By tapping in to these new authorities, the Department has been able to go on offense—to substantially expand America's information sharing capabilities. It enables us to get terrorist threat information quickly to our homeland security partners who need it most here on the front lines.

And the second is the investigative tools of the Patriot Act—many of which have been used for years to catch mafia dons and drug kingpins. Today those tools are being used by Homeland Security and other investigators across the country and overseas to identify, apprehend and stop terrorists before they can complete their plots.

The Roots of the Patriot Act

As many of you know, the roots of the Patriot Act trace back to 9/11 [the terrorist attacks of September 11, 2001]. When the Twin Towers crumbled to the ground, and the Pentagon burned, and the brave passengers of Flight 93 made their heroic good-byes in the skies here above Pennsylvania, I knew—we all knew—that we needed to think differently about how we would prevent another attack.

We needed a new philosophy—a philosophy of shared responsibility, shared leadership, and shared accountability. The integration of a nation.

Better information-sharing between agencies, as well as with our state and local partners, was a critical part of our new thinking, and critical to this integration. Like I said, prevention is our ultimate goal. To accomplish this goal requires, among other things, new tools and technologies. It requires a robust intelligence gathering operation. And it demands unprecedented information sharing and cooperation across all levels of government and the private sector.

Let me put this in context. Before September 11, intelligence officers and criminal investigators often couldn't share information with each other. In many cases—even just within the FBI—FBI intelligence officers and FBI criminal investigators couldn't share vital threat related information—even when they were right down the hall and working on the same terrorist cases. Our ability to fight terrorism was inhibited by the inability to coordinate within our own government.

But the Patriot Act helped change all that.

A Coordinated Campaign

The Patriot Act equips law enforcement and intelligence officials at the Department of Homeland Security and other Federal agencies with the tools we need to mount an effective, coordinated campaign against our nation's terrorist enemies.

The Patriot Act enables the kind of intelligence sharing necessary so that a complete picture of information can be compiled, so that first responders like the State troopers here today, can better understand what terrorists might be planning, and how to work together with us to prevent attacks.

Intelligence officers can now consult with federal law enforcement agents to coordinate efforts to investigate or protect against threats from foreign powers and their agents. This coordination between intelligence and law enforcement is vital to protecting the nation's security.

This increased ability to share information has directly led to the disruption of terrorist plots and numerous arrests, prosecutions, and convictions in terrorism cases, such as the "Lackawanna Six" up north near Buffalo, and the "Portland Seven" terrorist cell out in Oregon. Both involved cases in which the defendants went to Afghanistan or attempted to do so, to train or take up arms against America with Al Qaeda [terrorists].

We must continue to foster cooperation and information-sharing among national security and law enforcement personnel. We must continue dismantling roadblocks that prevent communication between the federal government and our partners like those here with us today in Pittsburgh.

We must do this because we must uncover terrorist plots before they are launched, and the Patriot Act is a critical part of this.

Providing Important Investigative Tools

But information sharing, by itself, is not enough. We also need the vital investigative tools of the Patriot Act, so that law enforcement officials on the front lines can do the job America expects of them.

We're talking about Homeland Security heroes like our Federal Air Marshals, who stand guard in the sky. Border Patrol officers on watch through the night, and the Coast Guard officers at sea, and the men and women of the United States Secret Service—one of the world's great law enforcement agencies. And yes the crack criminal investigators of ICE—Immigration & Customs Enforcement—today at the cutting edge of DHS enforcement capacity.

And let me tell you about one such ICE agent who stepped up and made a difference.

At the Miami International Airport not long ago, Homeland Security's Immigration and Customs Enforcement agents intercepted a money courier named Libardo Florez-Gomez. He was suspected of laundering an estimated $1.3 million per month for the Colombian leftist rebel group "FARC"—a group designated by the State Department as a foreign terrorist organization.

Thanks to Special Agent Norman Bright, an alert ICE agent who used his knowledge of key new elements of the Patriot Act in the investigation and interrogation, Florez-Gomez was arrested and charged with being an unlicensed money transmitter. His conviction [in 2003] demonstrates how the Patriot Act has helped to stem the flow of funds to terrorists by enhancing our ability to prosecute those responsible for funneling money to terrorists.

Winning the War on Terrorism

We are disrupting terrorist threats, and capturing the terrorists that would carry them out. Over the last two years:

- Our intelligence and law enforcement communities, and our partners, both here and abroad, have identified and disrupted over 150 terrorist threats and cells;
- Worldwide, nearly two-thirds of [the terrorist group] al Qaida's known senior leadership has been captured or killed—including a mastermind of the September 11th attacks;
- Worldwide, more than 3,000 operatives have been incapacitated;
- Four terrorist cells in Buffalo, Seattle, and Portland (Oregon), have been broken up;
- 357 individuals have been criminally charged in the United States in terrorism investigations;
- Already, 189 individuals have been convicted or have pled guilty in the United States, including shoe-bomber Richard Reid and "American Taliban" John Walker Lindh; and
- Over 515 individuals linked to the September 11th investigation have been removed from the United States.

Department of Justice, 2004. www.lifeandliberty.gov.

The work of Special Agent Bright and dozens of other cases in which Patriot Act provisions made a difference for America is included in a special new report that was sent to Congress. . . . It's an unprecedented compilation of real life cases from across the country in which law enforcement officials have used the tools of the USA PATRIOT Act to protect America's families and communities, and even to save lives.

Right here in Pennsylvania, for example, local police received a call in early 2002 that a 13-year-old girl had disappeared. She had been lured from her parents' home and was being held in chains, two states away, by a 38-year-old man she had met online. The clock was ticking. But thanks to Section 212 of the Patriot Act, federal agents here in Pittsburgh were able to quickly obtain the critical Internet evidence needed to locate the perpetrator and rescue the girl. The man was convicted and will spend most of the next 20 years in jail.

Unfortunately, the key information sharing provisions of the Patriot Act are under assault. Key information sharing provisions will expire [in 2005]. And there are those who would roll back some of the most critical investigative tools.

So let me state it plainly: The tools of the Patriot Act are vital to our ability to prevent terrorist attacks. It is not a zero sum game. Like the Department of Homeland Security and so many federal agencies, the authorities of the Patriot Act exist to protect the very liberties that our Founders established in the Constitution. By protecting our freedoms, our civil liberties are enhanced, not diminished.

A Team Effort

If we are truly going to be successful in protecting our country from those who wish to do us harm, the strategy must be a layered one—a series of tools designed to make sure homeland security professionals have the information they need to do their jobs—and to disrupt a potential attack before it can happen.

Homeland Security has not rested on the significant progress of the Patriot Act. Under President Bush's leadership we have also instituted other new initiatives to aid the flow of threat related information to state and local partners as well as the private sector.

The Homeland Security Information Network (HSIN) is one example of a new information sharing capability now in place. State and local officials brought it to us, told us, "This is a system that works, the demand is great, and we need it now." They were right.

So we worked with our state and local partners and established this real-time Internet collaboration system.

The Homeland Security Information Network allows multiple jurisdictions, disciplines, and emergency operation centers to receive and share the same intelligence and the same tactical information. Those who need to act on information now have the same overall situational awareness. And, as many of you in this room know, you now have this capability in Pittsburgh.

We are one team, with one mission: to prevent a terrorist attack.

The Department sees communication as a two-way process: we collect information from the field and listen to what you, our partners, need from us to do your jobs better. This means heightened awareness, better intelligence, wiser decisions, and improved coordination at every level.

The President has said, "The true strength of the country lies in the hearts and souls of our citizens." He is absolutely right. The federal government cannot micro-manage the protection of America. Instead, homeland security must become a priority in every city, every neighborhood, every home, and with every citizen.

One of the most important jobs at the Department of Homeland Security is to support local first responders in their pursuit of this mission with resources, training and new tools. Tools like the prime mover, equipment trailers, decontamination tents, and personal protective gear that Region 13 counties are receiving today.

I am pleased to report that you purchased this equipment using Department of Homeland Security grant money through our Office for Domestic Preparedness. . . .

Every day we work to make America more secure. Every day the memories of September 11 inspire us to live our vision, a vision to preserve our freedoms, protect America, enjoy our liberties and secure the homeland.

If there is one lesson we learned from 9-11, it is that freedom's greatest companion is fellowship; unity, the integration of a nation—everyone pledged to freedom's cause, everyone its protector, everyone its beneficiary.

Tools like the Patriot Act have put us on the right path. Our state and local partners have contributed to the success with good ideas such as the Homeland Security Information Network.

The key to the future lies with the continued success of new tools such as these and the commitment of people like you—our state and local partners across the country—to this all important mission.

"It is a mistake to believe that [the Patriot Act] marks a significant change in the way the government fights terrorism."

The Patriot Act Does Not Enhance National Security

John Yoo and Eric Posner

In the following viewpoint law professors John Yoo and Eric Posner contend that the Patriot Act simply expands the tools used during the Cold War to fight nation-states such as the Soviet Union and China and is thus inadequate to protect against terrorism. According to the authors, terrorist organizations are not organized like nation-states; they have no armies, infrastructure, or population to protect and can therefore act more boldly. Thus, the authors argue, the United States should consider strategies used by countries such as Israel, which have a history of fighting terrorism. Yoo teaches at the University of California, Berkeley, and Posner at the University of Chicago.

As you read, consider the following questions:
1. What 25-year-old statute do the central provisions of the Patriot Act modify, in the authors' opinion?
2. According to the authors, how did U.S. enemies operate in previous U.S. national security efforts?
3. What are some of the strategies that are often effective in countering terrorism, in the authors' view?

Years into the war against terrorism, the Patriot Act has become even more controversial than at its birth. Democratic presidential candidates have claimed that the law is unconstitutional and ought to be repealed, while Atty. Gen. John Ashcroft has barnstormed the country accusing its critics of zealotry and exaggeration. Civil liberties groups, such as the ACLU [American Civil Liberties Union], have brought lawsuits challenging the act's constitutionality. Cities have refused to cooperate with efforts to enforce the act.

Much of this controversy, however, is beside the point.

Although it cannot be denied that the Patriot Act expends government power to conduct surveillance of suspected terrorists within the United States, its central provisions only modify a 25-year-old statute, the Foreign Intelligence Surveillance Act [FISA]. FISA, not the Patriot Act, created the system of secret courts, classified hearings and secret warrants that allows the government to place covert wiretaps on or intercept the e-mails of those suspected of presenting a national security threat to the United States.

Changing Standards

The Patriot Act made only two significant changes to this regime: It changed the standard for granting a FISA warrant to allow law enforcement and intelligence personnel to cooperate more closely in using the fruits of FISA surveillance, and it brought within the warrant's reach tangible items, such as credit card receipts and banking records.

The Patriot Act's other modifications updated FISA for modern technologies, such as allowing surveillance of a single target suspect, rather than requiring a warrant for each individual phone line, cell phone and e-mail account.

These changes represent the evolutionary adaptation of existing laws to developments in international terrorism and technology. They are not a revolutionary effort to confront the challenges presented by the new terrorism revealed by the Sept. 11, 2001, attacks. No court has rejected these amendments, and, in fact, in 2002 a special court of federal appeals judges upheld the change in the FISA standard that allows more cooperation between the law-enforcement and intelligence communities.

While the Patriot Act makes useful improvements, it is a mistake to believe that it marks a significant change in the way the government fights terrorism. In fact, it may have the opposite effect by lulling us into an unwarranted sense of security.

Catching Spies

FISA was designed to counter Cold War espionage by the Soviet Union and its allies. Its surveillance provisions reflected concerns about foreign embassies and spies. Our political system's first legislative reaction to the threat posed by the Sept. 11 catastrophe, which demonstrated that a violent non-state terrorist organization could launch massive, surprise attacks on civilians within the United States, was merely to make amendments to a law designed to catch Soviet spies.

Military historians say that generals fight the last war. Politicians and government officials have the same problem.

The Patriot Act is the legal equivalent of the Maginot Line, a set of fixed defenses built by the French after World War I to stop a German invasion.

The French generals were trapped in an obsolete paradigm of military strategy. They expected World War I–style trench warfare, not the blitzkrieg that came. Rather than being trapped by Cold War ways of thinking, our political leaders should be considering new, revolutionary alternatives that directly address the threats posed by the new terrorism.

Previous U.S. national security efforts have been directed at nation states—such as the Soviet Union, and, before that, Germany, Italy and Japan—all of which fielded armed forces, defended territory and protected civilian populations. Our enemies operated as we did, attempting to expand their control over territory by military force or political coercion.

In contrast, Al Qaeda is a non-governmental organization with covert cells of operatives that hide among civilian populations and operate by launching surprise attacks to kill large numbers of civilians. They have no territory to defend, no population to protect, no infrastructure or armies in the field to attack. They are products of technologies, ideologies and global dynamics that were unknown when FISA was enacted 25 years ago.

But this kind of terrorism is not wholly unprecedented, and, in debating counterterrorism strategy, we should start by asking how other states have dealt with long-standing, serious terrorist problems. For example, Israeli counterterrorism strategies have included assassination, collective sanctions, including the demolition of the homes of suicide bombers, detention of suspects without charges for lengthy periods of time and aggressive interrogation techniques. Other liberal democracies, including Italy, Germany and Britain, have not gone as far, but have used similar strategies in their battles against terrorism.

Not So Foreign Strategies

While these strategies seem foreign to American traditions, news reports have suggested that U.S. forces have tried some of them in recent years. Targeted killings have been used against Al Qaeda and Iraqi military leaders. House demolitions have occurred in Iraq. Detentions without criminal charge have occurred in the United States, albeit mainly of illegal aliens. Aggressive interrogation techniques—includ-

Wasserman. © 2001 by *The Boston Globe*. Reproduced by permission of Tribune Media Services.

ing sleep deprivation and disorientation—reportedly have been used against captured Al Qaeda leaders abroad.

This kind of aggressive action has ample historical precedent.

In World War II, the United States targeted cities with the intention of killing thousands of civilians in order to demoralize the citizenry and undermine support for the government. American strategic doctrine during the Cold War treated the killings of millions of innocent Soviet citizens as an appropriate response to a Soviet first strike. In Vietnam, U.S. soldiers destroyed villages believed to be harboring Viet Cong.

The Success of Collective Sanctions

Collective sanctions are not just a military strategy; they have been used frequently during peacetime, though the tactic is known under the anodyne label of "economic sanctions." Economic sanctions against Iraq, for example, resulted in the deaths of thousands of innocent civilians. Though the suffering of Iraqi civilians was less visible, its purpose was no different from that of killing German and Japanese civilians during World War II.

The idea was to pressure citizens into withdrawing support for their governments.

Targeted killings, collective sanctions, preventive detention and aggressive interrogations often are effective in countering terrorism, but they also can fail. They might be abused, and they might backfire by generating public indignation at home and abroad.

Our point is not to recommend any of these measures but to shift the public debate away from the largely symbolic issues raised by the Patriot Act. The debate should instead focus on whether emergency measures used by other liberal democracies, and the United States in the past, are appropriate for the modern threat posed by Al Qaeda.

The Patriot Act debate reflects a mutual accommodation between left and right to avoid airing the challenges of the new terrorism.

Administration officials want to show that they have boldly confronted the terrorist threat; critics want a vehicle for asserting the value of civil liberties.

The debate may even be reassuring, because it reflects a politics-as-usual attitude that avoids the hard issues before us. But we need to move on. We need to think creatively about strategies and tactics for the new war we have before us, not the one we had 120 years ago.

"If we knew then what we know now, we would have passed the Patriot Act six months before September 11th rather than six weeks after the attacks."

The Patriot Act Was Necessary

John Ashcroft

In the following viewpoint U.S. attorney general John Ashcroft argues that America's national security policies contained fatal flaws prior to the Patriot Act, which was signed into law shortly after the terrorist attacks of September 11, 2001. A wall between law enforcement and intelligence communities prevented the interagency communication and coordination needed to prevent terrorist plots, he maintains. Moreover, Ashcroft claims, terrorists exploited the fact that U.S. law enforcement relied on outdated technology. According to Ashcroft, the Patriot Act remedies these flaws so that all agencies charged with national security can act as an antiterror team, using the most advanced intelligence tools available.

As you read, consider the following questions:

1. According to Ashcroft, how did Congress, by passing the Patriot Act, begin to tear down the walls between intelligence and law enforcement officials?
2. What evidence does the author provide to support his contention that the Patriot Act expands the capabilities of Joint Terrorism Task Forces?
3. What would happen if the technological tools provided by the Patriot Act were abandoned, in the author's view?

John Ashcroft, address to the American Enterprise Institute, Washington, DC, August 19, 2003.

[O]n August 19, 2003], terrorists struck the United Nations mission in Baghdad, [Iraq] killing at least 13 people and seriously injuring at least 120 others. The victims were innocent people who traveled to Iraq on a mission of peace and human dignity. Let me express sympathy to the victims and their loved ones.

This morning's attack again confirms that the worldwide terrorist threat is real and imminent. Our enemies continue to pursue ways to murder the innocent and the peaceful. They seek to kill us abroad and at home. But we will not be deterred from our responsibility to preserve American life and liberty, nor our duty to build a safer, more secure world. . . .

Gaining Necessary Tools

Where a culture of law-enforcement inhibition prevented communication and coordination, we have built a new ethos of justice, one rooted in cooperation, nurtured by coordination, and focused on a single, overarching goal: the prevention of terrorist attacks. All of this has been done within the safeguards of our Constitution and its guarantees of protection for American freedom.

When terrorists had bested us with technology, communications, and information, we fought for the tools necessary to preserve the lives and liberty of the American people.

In the long winter of 1941, [British prime minister] Winston Churchill appealed to the United States for help in defending freedom from Nazism with the phrase, "Give us the tools and we will finish the job." In the days after, [the September 11, 2001, terrorist attacks], we appealed to Congress for help in defending freedom from terrorism with the same refrain: "Give us the tools and we will finish the job."

Congress responded by passing the USA Patriot Act by an overwhelming margin. And while our job is not finished, we have used the tools provided in the Patriot Act to fulfill our first responsibility to protect the American people. We have used these tools to prevent terrorists from unleashing more death and destruction on our soil. We have used these tools to save innocent American lives. We have used these tools to provide the security that ensures liberty.

Today, almost two years from the day of the [terrorist attacks of September 11], we know more than ever before about our capacity to defend ourselves from terrorists. We know now that there were fatal flaws in our national defenses prior to September 11. We know now that al-Qaeda understood these flaws. And we know now that al-Qaeda exploited the flaws in our defenses to murderous effect.

Two years later, the evidence is clear: If we knew then what we know now, we would have passed the Patriot Act six months before September 11th rather than six weeks after the attacks.

For Congress to have done less would have been a failure of government's most basic responsibility to the American people . . . to preserve life and liberty.

For Congress to have done less would have ignored the lethal lessons taught that tragic day in September.

Congress . . . completed an 18-month study of the causes of September 11th. Congress's conclusion . . . that there was a need for better communication, a need for better cooperation, a need for prevention . . . read like a preamble to the Patriot Act written two years after the hard lessons of history.

A Lack of Communication

First, the report found that prior to September 11th intelligence agencies and law enforcement failed to communicate with each other about terrorist hijackers . . . even those identified as suspects. This lack of communications had its roots deep in the culture of government. The walls between those who gather intelligence and those who enforce the laws prevented action that could save lives.

Fortunately, in the Patriot Act, Congress began to tear down the walls that cut off communication between intelligence and law enforcement officials. The Patriot Act gave agencies like the FBI and the CIA the ability to integrate their capabilities. It gave government the ability to "connect the dots," revealing the shadowy terrorist network in our midst.

In Portland, Oregon, we have indicted several persons for allegedly conspiring to travel to Afghanistan after the September 11th attacks in an effort to fight against American forces. In an example of excellent information-sharing between local, state, and federal authorities, the investigation began when a local sheriff in another state shared with the Portland Joint Terrorism Task Force information one of his deputies had developed from a traffic stop.

Because the investigation involved both intelligence techniques and law enforcement tools, the Patriot Act's elimination of the "wall" was critical in allowing all of the dots to be connected and the criminal charges to be fully developed. Recently one of the defendants, Maher Hawash, pled guilty to illegally providing support to the Taliban [regime in Afghanistan, which supported al-Qaeda] and agreed to cooperate with the government. He faces a sentence of seven to ten years in prison.

Using Outdated Technology

Second, the congressional report on September 11th found that U.S. law enforcement had long been forced to rely on outdated and insufficient technology in its efforts to prevent terrorist attacks.

Fortunately, in the Patriot Act, Congress gave law enforcement improved tools to prevent terrorism in the age of high technology. For example, where before investigators were forced to get a different wiretap order every time a suspect changed cell phones, now investigators can get a single wiretap that applies to the suspect and various phones he uses.

Thanks to the Patriot Act, we may deploy technology to track and develop cases against alleged terrorist operatives.

Uzir Paracha was a Pakistani national living in New York, who allegedly met an al-Qaeda operative overseas. Paracha allegedly agreed to help procure United States immigration documents, deposit money in a U.S. bank account, and use a post office box, all to allegedly facilitate the al-Qaeda operative's clandestine arrival in this country.

Paracha was charged on August 8 [2003] with conspiracy to provide material support to al-Qaeda.

A Lack of Cooperation

Third, the congressional report on September 11th determined that there was not enough cooperation among federal, state, and local law enforcement to combat a terrorist threat that found safe haven in the most nondescript of communities.

Fortunately, the Patriot Act expanded the capabilities of our Joint Terrorism Task Forces, which combine federal, state and local law enforcement officers into a seamless anti-terror team with international law enforcement and intelligence agencies.

A Wall Between Foreign Intelligence and Domestic Law Enforcement

Before the Patriot Act, FISA [Foreign Intelligence Surveillance Act] warrants were issued upon a showing that the "primary purpose" of the surveillance was to gather foreign intelligence information. Both the Department of Justice and the special FISA court that issued the warrants interpreted this language, for reasons known only to themselves, to mean that any such information gathered by counter-intelligence services could not be shared, except under rare circumstances, with [domestic] law enforcement officials. This "wall" prevented law enforcement officials and counter-intelligence officials from pooling their information—a dangerous and stupid practice given that [the terrorist group] al Qaeda has demonstrated that terrorists can easily operate outside and inside the United States.

Eric Posner and John Yoo, *Wall Street Journal*, December 9, 2003.

Hemant Lakhani is an alleged arms dealer in Great Britain, who is charged with attempting to sell shoulder-fired missiles to terrorists for use against American targets. After a long undercover investigation in several countries, Lakhani traveled to Newark, New Jersey, . . . and was arrested, along with two alleged financial facilitators, as he allegedly prepared to finalize the sale of the first missile.

The Lakhani investigation would not have been possible had American, Russian and other foreign intelligence and law enforcement agencies not been able to coordinate and communicate the intelligence they had gained from various investigative tools.

To address all of the issues surrounding the Patriot Act would require more time than we have here. It is critical, however, for everyone to understand what the Patriot Act means for our success in the war against terrorism. I would encourage Americans to take a few minutes and log on to a new web site, www.lifeandliberty.gov. There, you can read about the Patriot Act, read what members of Congress and others have said about the Patriot Act, and find out how it is keeping our nation safe and secure.

Armed with the tools provided by the Patriot Act, the men and women of justice and law enforcement have dedicated themselves to the unfinished work of those who resisted, those who assisted, and those who sacrificed on September 11th.

We have neutralized alleged terrorist cells in Buffalo, Detroit, Seattle and Portland.

To date, we have brought 255 criminal charges. One hundred thirty-two individuals have been convicted or pled guilty.

All told, more than 3,000 suspected terrorists have been arrested in many countries. Many more have met a different fate.

We have worked hard, but we have not labored alone:

Our efforts have been supported by Republicans and Democrats in Congress.

Our efforts have been ratified by the courts in legal challenge after legal challenge.

Our efforts have been rewarded by the trust of the American people. A two to one majority of Americans believe the Patriot Act is a necessary and effective tool that protects liberty, because it targets terrorists. Ninety-one percent of Americans understand that the Patriot Act has not affected their civil rights or the civil rights of their families.

What We Now Know

The painful lessons of September 11th remain touchstones, reminding us of government's responsibility to its people. Those lessons have directed us down a path that preserves life and liberty.

Almost two years after Americans fought in the skies over Shanksville,[1] [Pennsylvania] we know that communication

---

1. The author refers to Flight 93, which crashed in a field near Johnstown, Pennsylvania. The facts remain disputed, but evidence shows that some of the passengers took control of the plane and stopped the terrorists from using it as another weapon on September 11, 2001.

works. The Patriot Act opened opportunities for information sharing. To abandon this tool would disconnect the dots, risk American lives and liberty, and reject September 11th's lessons.

Almost two years after Americans died at the Pentagon, we know that cooperation works. The Patriot Act creates teamwork at every level of law enforcement and intelligence. To block cooperation against terrorists would make our nation more vulnerable to attack and reject the teachings of September 11th. Almost two years after Americans and the citizens of more than 80 other nations died at the World Trade Center we know that prevention works. The Patriot Act gives us the technological tools to anticipate, adapt and out-think our terrorist enemy. To abandon these tools would senselessly imperil American lives and American liberty, and ignore the lessons of September 11th.

The cause we have chosen is just. The course we have chosen is constitutional. The course we have chosen is preserving lives. For two years Americans have been safe. Because we are safer, our liberties are more secure.

"The administration . . . had the right 'tools' in place before Sept. 11."

The Patriot Act Was Unnecessary

Peter Erlinder

The Bush administration had the intelligence tools needed to fight terrorism before the attacks of September 11, 2001, but it failed to use them, claims Peter Erlinder in the following viewpoint. Nevertheless, he contends, the administration used this failure to justify the passing of the Patriot Act, which sacrifices civil liberties for increases in executive power. Since Congress passed the act not knowing that tools to fight terrorism were already available, Erlinder argues, the act should be repealed. Erlinder, law professor at William Mitchell College of Law, in St. Paul, Minnesota, is former president of the National Lawyers Guild.

As you read, consider the following questions:

1. In Erlinder's view, what can't the Bush administration's "lack of specific warnings" defense explain away?
2. What has happened to members of Congress who question administration policy, in Erlinder's opinion?
3. According to the author, what has happened at the local level in response to the terrorist attacks and the subsequent Patriot Act?

The storm of questions and criticism following revelations that the Bush administration had numerous warnings of an impending hijacking before the Sept. 11 [2001 terrorist attack] have focused primarily on the Nixon-era mantra, "What did he know, and when did he know it?" But even if a congressional investigation agrees with Bush administration protestations that the warnings weren't specific enough to know what to do, administration policy after Sept. 11 is going to require some explaining, too.

Justifying a Power Grab

The "lack of specific warnings" defense may justify a lack of action before the airliners hit the World Trade Center, but it can't explain away the lies that were told to Congress and the American people after Sept. 11 to justify the administration's war on civil liberties. The administration has been cynically using its own failure to act on intelligence developed under then-existing laws to justify vastly increasing its own power at the expense of civil freedoms.

Within a month of Sept. 11, Attorney General John Ashcroft packaged an old FBI wish list as the USA Patriot Act and demanded Congress pass it without discussion, because of the threat of yet another "Pearl Harbor-like attack." He told us the administration needed new "tools" to prevent unexpected terrorist attacks—new wiretap authority; secret searches; the use of secret evidence; secret immigration hearings; taping lawyers' conversations; locking up "undesirables" on his command, and other measures.

No less an expert than Supreme Court Justice Sandra Day O'Connor told us that concerns about civil liberties and abuse of power had to be shelved because of the "unexpected" new threat. Members of Congress have been accused of being the next thing to traitors for questioning administration policy and have even been forcibly expelled from Ashcroft's secret immigration hearings. Thousands have been locked up and deported, though no terrorists have been found, and our allies object to our holding of prisoners in violation of international law.

By presidential decree, the press has been cut off from normal access to government information. Local law en-

No Pre-Patriot Act Wall Between Intelligence and Law Enforcement

The [Joint Intelligence Community–Law Enforcement Working Group] found that there were far fewer legal impediments to information sharing between the law enforcement and intelligence communities than many people in both communities had thought, and that the principal obstacles were ones of agency culture and lack of understanding. There are simply no walls or restrictions on sharing the vast majority of counterterrorism information. There are no legal restrictions at all on the ability of members of the intelligence community to share intelligence information with each other. With respect to sharing between intelligence investigators and criminal investigators, information learned as a result of a physical surveillance or from a confidential informant can be legally shared without restriction.

Janet Reno, testimony before the National Commission on Terrorist Attacks Upon the United States, April 13, 2004.

---

forcement is being deputized for federal immigration duty and Ashcroft is indicting lawyers who represent alleged terrorists a bit too independently. Even at the state level, in places like Minnesota, local law enforcement has gotten on the bandwagon with state "antiterrorism" bills that ape the Ashcroft proposals.

All of this has been justified in the name of preventing another "surprise attack." The administration, however, had the right "tools" in place before Sept. 11. Those tools would have proved effective, if the administration had known how to use them.

Now we know that we were all deceived. Recent revelations about the Sept. 11 tragedy prove that existing investigative powers were effective. The Bush administration used its own failure to act on the warnings it had received to justify grabbing even more power, at the expense of our civil liberties, by deceiving Congress and the American people.

The USA Patriot Act became law in less than a month, without any hearings. Now that we know it was passed under false pretenses, Congress should repeal it just as quickly. And the Bush administration should rescind the policies that diminish our civil liberties, until we can get an honest assessment of what went wrong in the months before Sept. 11.

> *"Hundreds of foreign criminals and
> suspected terrorists, plus one known
> member of [the terrorist group] al Qaeda,
> were prevented from entering the
> country."*

Patriot Act Immigration Provisions Enhance National Security

Michelle Malkin

The immigration provisions of the Patriot Act, crafted primarily by Assistant Attorney General Viet Dinh, himself an immigrant, have successfully enhanced national security, argues Michelle Malkin in the following viewpoint. The act helps the government monitor the entry and exit of foreign students and aids in the tracking of nonimmigrant visitors from the Middle East, she claims. These provisions have led to the arrest and conviction of suspected terrorists and have prevented terrorist plots, Malkin asserts. Malkin is a nationally syndicated columnist for Creators Syndicate.

As you read, consider the following questions:

1. What is the most important antiterrorism policy that Viet Dinh and his colleagues designed, in Malkin's view?
2. According to the author, to what do critics hysterically compare the detention of illegal aliens from terror-friendly countries?
3. What, in the author's opinion, is Edmund Burke's theory of "Ordered Liberty"?

To civil-liberties alarmists, Viet Dinh is a traitor. To me, he is an American hero.

Dinh, 35, is widely known—and reviled—as the primary architect of the Patriot Act. Until May [2003], he was an assistant attorney general for the Office of Legal Policy in John Ashcroft's Justice Department. (He stepped down to return to his law school post at Georgetown University.) Since the Sept. 11 [2001] terrorist attacks, Dinh told *The Christian Science Monitor*, "our nation's ability to defend itself against terror has been not only my vocation but my obsession."

[During the 2003] Fourth of July holiday, I will give thanks for those like Dinh who have worked tirelessly to ensure domestic tranquility, provide for the common defense, and secure the blessings of liberty that no other country in the world can match.

Enforcing the Law

A constitutional law expert, Dinh's office had been mostly concerned with judicial nominations before Sept. 11. After the mass murder of 3,000 men, women and children on American soil, Dinh became an instrumental member of the brain trust that designed the Bush administration's anti-terrorism policies. Most importantly, the Patriot Act revised outdated rules that fatally hampered surveillance of suspected terrorists in America. Dinh also helped craft plans to monitor the entry and exit of foreign students and to register and track non-immigrant visitors from high-risk Middle Eastern countries.

An immigrant himself who escaped from communist Vietnam a quarter-century ago aboard a rickety boat, Dinh notes that foreign visitors to our shores are guests obligated to obey the laws—some which "have not been enforced for 50 years." It was time, Dinh and his colleagues decided, to start enforcing them.

The results speak for themselves:

- The feds have busted more than 20 suspected al Qaeda [terrorist] cell members from Buffalo, N.Y., to Detroit, Seattle, and Portland, Ore.
- More than 100 other individuals have been convicted or pled guilty to terrorist related crimes.

Answering Patriot Act Critics

Wired News spoke to [assistant attorney general Viet] Dinh about the Patriot Act and its effect on the liberties of American citizens. . . .

Wired News: An estimated 5,000 people have been subjected to detention since [the September 11, 2001, terrorist attacks]. Of those, only five—three noncitizens and two citizens—were charged with terrorism-related crimes and one was convicted. How do we justify such broad-sweeping legislation that has resulted in very few terrorist-related convictions?

Viet Dinh: I've heard the 5,000 number. The official numbers released from the Department of Justice indicate approximately 500 persons have been charged with immigration violations and have been deported who have been of interest to the 9/11 investigation. Also, approximately 300 individuals have been criminally charged who are of interest to the 9/11 investigation. Of the persons criminally charged, approximately half have either pled guilty or been convicted after trial.

It may well be that a number of citizens were not charged with terrorism-related crimes, but they need not be. Where the department has suspected people of terrorism it will prosecute those persons for other violations of law, rather than wait for a terrorist conspiracy to fully develop and risk the potential that that conspiracy will be missed and thereby sacrificing innocent American lives in the process.

Kim Zetler, *Wired*, February 24, 2004.

- The United States has deported 515 individuals linked to the Sept. 11 investigation.
- Hundreds of foreign criminals and suspected terrorists, plus one known member of al Qaeda, were prevented from entering the country thanks to the National Entry-Exit Registration System—which Sen. Ted Kennedy attempted to sabotage.
- Long overdue fingerprint cross checks of immigration and FBI databases at the border have resulted in the arrest of more than 5,000 fugitives, wanted for crimes committed in the United States.
- And nearly two years after the Sept. 11 attacks, there has not yet been another mass terrorist attack on our homeland.

Opponents of the Bush administration's homeland defense and immigration enforcement efforts complain that the war on terror has eviscerated civil liberties and constitutional rights. They have falsely portrayed the Patriot Act as allowing the feds to spy on library patrons without a warrant or criminal suspicion—a lie perpetuated by the truth-challenged *New York Times.*

They have hysterically compared the detention of illegal aliens from terror-friendly countries to the World War II internment of Japanese. And they have likened Ashcroft, Dinh, and the Justice Department to the Taliban[1] and Nazis. Never mind that the courts have so far upheld every major initiative and tactic from keeping immigration deportation hearings closed, to maintaining secrecy of the names of illegal alien detainees, to allowing use of the Patriot Act surveillance powers.

Dinh is refreshingly unapologetic and to the point in response to the alarmists: "The threat to liberty comes from Osama bin Laden and his terrorist network, not from the men and women in blue who work to uphold the law." Drawing on Edmund Burke's theory of "Ordered Liberty," which argues that liberty cannot be exercised unless government has first provided civil order, Dinh observes: "I think security exists for liberty to flourish and liberty cannot exist without order and security."

On July 4th, this fundamental lesson of Sept. 11 must not be forgotten. The charred earth, mangled steel, crashing glass, fiery chaos and eviscerated bodies are indelible reminders that the blessings of liberty in America do not secure themselves.

1. The Taliban is a fundamentalist Islamic regime that took over Afghanistan in 1996.

> *"What we have done is to sacrifice the liberties of some . . . for the purported security of the rest of us."*

The Patriot Act Unfairly Targets Immigrants to Enhance National Security

David Cole

In the following viewpoint David Cole argues that the Patriot Act unfairly sacrifices immigrants' rights to enhance national security. The act makes immigrants deportable for having even a minor association with a terrorist organization, claims Cole, and grants the government broad power to detain immigrants for an unspecified time without a hearing, which violates their right to due process. Moreover, these detentions are not subject to judicial review, and the government refuses to disclose information on those detained, he contends. Cole, a constitutional law professor at Georgetown University, is author of *Enemy Aliens*.

As you read, consider the following questions:
1. According to Cole, how has the Supreme Court reasoned that guilt by association violates the First and Fifth Amendments?
2. In the author's opinion, how does the Patriot Act resurrect ideological exclusion?
3. Who might be included in the broad definition of a "suspected terrorist," in the author's view?

David Cole, "Terrorizing Immigrants in the Name of Fighting Terrorism," *Human Rights*, vol. 29, Winter 2002. Copyright © 2002 by The American Bar Association. Reproduced by permission.

It is often said that civil liberties are the first casualties of war. It may be more accurate to say that *immigrants'* civil liberties are the first to go. In the wake of the devastating terrorist attacks of September 11 [2001], we all feel vulnerable in ways that we have never felt before, and many have argued that we may need to sacrifice our liberty in order to purchase security. In fact, however, what we have done is to sacrifice the liberties of some—immigrants, and especially Arab and Muslim immigrants—for the purported security of the rest of us. This double standard is an all too tempting way to strike the balance—it allows citizens to enjoy a sense of security without sacrificing their own liberty, but it is an illegitimate trade-off. In the end, moreover, it is likely to be counterproductive, as it will alienate the very communities that we most need to work with as we fight the war on terrorism. . . .

Guilt by Association

The problems begin with the USA Patriot Act (Patriot Act), enacted in haste under threats from Attorney General John Ashcroft that if another terrorist incident occurred before the law was signed, Congress would be held responsible. Among other things, it imposes guilt by association on immigrants, a philosophy that the Supreme Court has condemned as "alien to the traditions of a free society and the First Amendment itself." Before the advent of the Patriot Act, aliens were deportable for engaging in or supporting *terrorist activity*. The Patriot Act makes them deportable for virtually any *associational activity* with a "terrorist organization," irrespective of whether the alien's support has any connection to an act of violence, much less terrorism. And because the Act defines "terrorist activity" to include virtually any use or threat to use a weapon against a person or property, and defines a "terrorist organization" as any group of two or more persons that engages in such an act, the proscription on political association potentially encompasses every organization that has ever been involved in a civil war or a crime of violence, from a pro-life group that once threatened workers at an abortion clinic, to the ANC [African National Congress], the IRA [Irish Republican Army], or the Northern Alliance in Afghanistan.

Once a group is designated as a "terrorist group," aliens are deportable for asking people to join it, fundraising for it, or providing any kind of material support to it, including dues. Indeed, the law extends even to those who support a group in an effort to *counter* terrorism. Thus, an immigrant who offered his services in peace negotiating to the IRA in the hope of furthering the peace process in Great Britain could be deported as a terrorist.

This is guilt by association, because it treats aliens as culpable not for their own acts, but for the acts of those with whom their conduct is associated. Guilt by association, the Supreme Court has ruled, violates the First and Fifth Amendments. All people in the United States have a First Amendment right to associate with groups that have lawful and unlawful ends, so long as they do not further the group's illegal ends. And the Fifth Amendment dictates that "in our jurisprudence guilt is personal." Without some connection between the alien's support and terrorist activity, the Constitution is violated.

Some argue that the threat from terrorist organizations abroad requires compromise on the principle prohibiting guilt by association. But this constitutional principle was developed in connection with measures directed at the Communist Party, an organization that Congress found to be a foreign-dominated organization that used sabotage and terrorism for the purpose of overthrowing the United States by force and violence, and that was supported by the world's other great superpower.

Others argue that money is fungible, so support of a group's lawful activities will simply free up resources that will be spent on terrorism. But that argument proves too much, for it would authorize guilt by association whenever any organization engages in some illegal activity. Donations to the Democratic Party, it could be argued, "free up" resources that are used to violate campaign finance laws, yet surely we could not criminalize all support to the Democratic Party simply because it sometimes violates the campaign finance laws. Moreover, the fungibility argument assumes that every marginal dollar provided to a designated group will, in fact, be spent on violence. However, no one would seriously contend that every dollar given to the ANC for its lawful anti-apartheid work freed up a dollar that was spent on that organization's terrorist activity.

Ideological Exclusion

The Patriot Act also resurrects ideological exclusion, the practice of denying entry to aliens for pure speech. It excludes aliens who "endorse or espouse terrorist activity," or who "persuade others to support terrorist activity or a terrorist organization," in ways that the secretary of state determines undermine U.S. efforts to combat terrorism. It also excludes aliens who are representatives of groups that "endorse acts of terrorist activity" in ways that similarly undermine U.S. efforts to combat terrorism.

Excluding people for their ideas is flatly contrary to the spirit of freedom for which the United States stands. It was for that reason that Congress repealed all such grounds in the Immigration and Nationality Act in 1990, after years of embarrassing politically motivated visa denials. We are a strong enough country, and our resolve against terrorism is powerful enough, to make such censorship wholly unnecessary.

Detention Versus Due Process

The government has detained well over 1,200 persons in connection with the investigation of the attacks of September 11. (The DOJ [Department of Justice] has halted its practice of publicizing the total number detained so we don't know how much higher the actual figure may be.) As of December 2001, over 500 persons were still being held in federal custody, with an untold number of others being held in state and local custody. Yet, as of that same time, only one person had been charged with involvement in the crimes perpetrated that day—Zaccarias Moussaoui. Department of Justice officials claim that about ten or twelve of the detained may be linked to Al Qaeda, but of course that only raises a question about the rest. The DOJ has been unwilling to disclose even the most basic information about the largest group of detainees, those held on immigration charges. It refuses even to identify who is detained. The immigrants are being tried in secret proceedings, closed to the public, the press, or even family members. Immigration judges are instructed not to list the cases on the docket, and to refuse to confirm or deny that cases even exist. Such practices are unprecedented. But what we do know, mostly from enterprising investigative journalists, suggests that the vast majority have all but the most attenuated connections to the events of that terrible day. Most of those detained appear to be Arabs or Muslims.

Bulbul. © 2003 by Bulbul. Reproduced by permission of Arachne Publishing.

The administration has dramatically changed the rules governing its authority to detain immigrants. Shortly after September 11, the INS unilaterally amended a regulation governing detention without charges. The regulation had required the INS to file charges within twenty-four hours of detaining an alien; under the new regulations, detention without charges is permissible for forty-eight hours, and for an unspecified "reasonable" period beyond forty-eight hours in times of emergency.

Before September 11, the INS could detain any alien placed in removal proceedings for as long as the proceedings lasted—in many cases several years. However, it could do so only if it had reason to believe that he or she posed a threat to national security or a risk of flight, and the alien was entitled to seek release from an immigration judge. Under a new regulation, however, even if the immigration judge rules that the alien should be released, INS prosecutors can keep him locked up simply by filing an appeal of the release order. They need not make any showing that their appeal is likely to succeed. Appeals of immigration custody decisions routinely take months and often more than a year to decide.

A Broad Definition

The Patriot Act goes still further, giving the attorney general unilateral authority to detain aliens on his say-so, without any opportunity for the alien to respond to the charges. The attorney general may detain any immigrant whom he certifies as a "suspected terrorist." The Patriot Act defines a "suspected terrorist" so broadly that it includes virtually every immigrant who has been involved in a barroom brawl or domestic dispute, as well as aliens who have never committed an act of violence in their life, and whose only crime is that he or she provided humanitarian aid to an organization disfavored by the government.

This provision raises several basic constitutional concerns. It mandates preventive detention of persons who pose no threat to national security or risk of flight, and without any hearing. And it allows the INS to detain such aliens *indefinitely*, even where they prevail in their removal proceedings. This is akin to detaining a prisoner even after he has been pardoned.

The provision permits certification and detention on mere "reasonable grounds to believe" that an alien has engaged in terrorist activity, a standard that the INS has likened to the "reasonable suspicion" required for a brief stop and frisk under the Fourth Amendment. But under the Fourth Amendment, "reasonable suspicion" does not even

53

justify a custodial arrest, much less indefinite detention.

The provision also permits detention for up to seven days without filing any charges. Yet, the Supreme Court has ruled in the criminal setting that charges must be filed within forty-eight hours except in the most extraordinary circumstances. In short, hundreds of immigrants not charged with any crime, much less involvement in the September 11 attack, are being detained in secret, even where judges rule that there is no basis for detention, and without going before a judge at all. . . .

There is good reason to doubt whether these measures will in fact make us safer. By penalizing even wholly lawful, nonviolent, and counter-terrorist associational activity, we are likely to waste valuable resources tracking innocent political activity, drive other activity underground, encourage extremists, and make the communities that will inevitably be targeted by such measures far less likely to cooperate with law enforcement. And by conducting law enforcement in secret, and jettisoning procedures designed to protect the innocent and afford legitimacy to the outcome of trials, we will encourage people to fear the worst about our government. As Justice Louis Brandeis wrote nearly seventy-five years ago, the framers of our Constitution knew "that fear breeds repression; that repression breeds hate; and that hate menaces stable government." In other words, freedom and security need not necessarily be traded off against one another; maintaining our freedoms is itself critical to maintaining our security.

"The USA PATRIOT Act . . . strengthened the criminal laws against terrorism by making it easier to prosecute those responsible for funneling money to terrorists."

The Patriot Act Reduces Terrorist Financing

U.S. Department of Justice

According to the U.S. Department of Justice in the following viewpoint, the Patriot Act prevents terrorist plots by strengthening criminal laws against those who give financial assistance to terrorists. The Patriot Act, the department maintains, has made giving any aid to terrorists, including funneling money to terrorist organizations, a crime with a substantial penalty. As a result, the authors contend, the U.S. Department of Justice has been able to disable many terrorist plots.

As you read, consider the following questions:

1. In the opinion of the Department of Justice, what was missing in pre-Patriot Act definitions of "material support"?
2. According to the authors, how did the Patriot Act help law enforcement authorities arrest and charge terrorist money launderer Libardo Florez-Gomez?
3. In the authors' view, how did the Patriot Act change the punishment for bulk cash smuggling?

U.S. Department of Justice, *Report from the Field: The USA Patriot Act at Work*, July 2004.

The USA PATRIOT Act is one aspect of the [Justice] Department's overarching strategy to remove terrorists from the streets. The Department aims to use its prosecutorial discretion—investigating, prosecuting, and punishing crimes that in the past might have been overlooked—in order to incapacitate suspected terrorists and thereby prevent terrorist attacks. The Act has enhanced the Department's ability to pursue this strategy by strengthening the nation's criminal laws against terrorism, providing the Department with a solid foundation to pursue what has become the Department's highest priority.

For example, before the Act, it was a federal crime to provide material support to individuals or organizations that commit various terrorism crimes. The definition of "material support," however, did not clearly include providing expert advice and assistance—for example, a civil engineer's advice on how to destroy a building or a biochemist's advice on how to make a biological agent more lethal. The law also did not explicitly state that providing "monetary instruments" to a designated foreign terrorist organization constituted material support. Section 805 of the USA PATRIOT Act bolstered the ban on providing material support to terrorists by clearly making it a crime to provide terrorists with "expert advice or assistance" and by clarifying that "material support" includes all forms of money, not just hard currency. In addition, section 810 increased the maximum penalty for providing material support to a terrorist or a terrorist organization from 10 years to 15 years in prison. The Department has successfully used the material support statute in a number of recent cases, such as those involving terror cells in Lackawanna, New York and Virginia. Between September 11, 2001 and May 5, 2004, the Department charged over 50 defendants with material support offenses in 17 different judicial districts.

Terrorist Financing

The USA PATRIOT Act also strengthened the criminal laws against terrorism by making it easier to prosecute those responsible for funneling money to terrorists. Under previous federal law, 18 U.S.C. § 1960, those who operated unlicensed money transmitting businesses were entitled to rely on the affirmative defense that they had no knowledge of applicable state licensing requirements. Some of these businesses, called hawalas, have funneled extensive amounts of money to terrorist groups abroad. Section 373 of the USA PATRIOT Act amended federal law by eliminating this loophole requiring that the defendant know about state licensing requirements and also by broadening the statute to make it illegal for a person to transmit or transport funds that are the proceeds of criminal activity or funds that are intended to be used for criminal activity. This improved statute has been used in numerous federal prosecutions.

Prosecutors in Florida used section 373 to charge Libardo Florez-Gomez, a money courier who, based upon documentation found on his person, was suspected of laundering an estimated $1.3 million per month for the Revolutionary Armed Forces of Colombia ("FARC"), a leftist rebel group designated by the State Department as a foreign terrorist organization. After intercepting him at the Miami International Airport with $182,000 in euros, U.S. Immigration & Customs Enforcement agents learned during an interview with Florez-Gomez that he intended to convert the euros to dollars in Miami and then transfer them to unknown bank accounts. Because Florez-Gomez was in the business of money transmission, he was arrested and charged with being an unlicensed money transmitter in violation of 18 U.S.C. § 1960, as amended by section 373 of the USA PATRIOT Act. On April 3, 2003, Florez-Gomez pleaded guilty and was subsequently sentenced to serve 18 months in prison, followed by two years of supervised release, and required to forfeit $151,000. In this case, the U.S. Immigration & Customs Enforcement agent who investigated Florez-Gomez was familiar with the statutory registration requirements for money transmitting, which prompted him to focus his interrogation of Florez-Gomez on details pertinent to that violation and not on the elusive element of Florez-Gomez's "knowledge" of the registration requirements—as would have been required prior to enactment of the USA PATRIOT Act.

Prosecutors in New Jersey have used section 373 of the USA PATRIOT Act to bring charges against Yehuda Abraham, an unlicensed money transmitter whose services were used by Hemant Lakhani, an individual attempting to sell shoulder-fired surface-to-air missiles to terrorists with the understanding that they were going to be used to shoot down American commercial airliners. Lakhani employed Abraham's money transmitting services to funnel, from the United States to an overseas account, money being paid by a cooperating witness, acting under the direction of federal law enforcement officers, as a down payment on the first missile. As a result of the USA PATRIOT Act, prosecutors were able to quickly put together an effective case against Abraham for operating an unlicensed money transmitting business, avoiding the often fatal issues that plagued such cases prior to the passage of the USA PATRIOT Act. As a result of the strength of the case against him, Abraham entered a plea of guilty to a violation of 18 U.S.C. § 1960 on March 30, 2004. At sentencing, Abraham could receive up to 37 months imprisonment and a $250,000 fine.

Prosecutors have also secured convictions of individuals operating unlicensed money transmitting businesses that sent money from the United States to Iraq, Yemen, the United Arab Emirates, and India. In Boston, for example, the successful prosecution of Mohammed Hussein, the co-operator of an al-Barakaat-affiliated money transmitting business, was based on both pre- and post-USA PATRIOT Act violations of 18 U.S.C. § 1960. In 2000 and 2001, Barakaat accepted approximately $3 million in customer deposits and wired those funds to the United Arab Emirates without a license. Based on those transactions, Hussein was sentenced on July 22, 2002, to one-and-a-half years in prison, to be followed by two years of supervised release.

Criminalizing Bulk Cash Smuggling

In an effort to stem the flow of money to terrorists, section 371 of the USA PATRIOT Act made bulk cash smuggling a serious criminal offense. Section 371 specifically forbids concealing more than $10,000 in currency or other monetary instruments and transporting it out of or into the United States with the intent to evade relevant reporting requirements. Violators are subject to five years in prison and forfeiture of any property involved in the offense. Prior to the passage of the USA PATRIOT Act, federal law required anyone transporting monetary instruments of more than $10,000 into or out of the country to file a report but did not make currency smuggling itself a crime. The U.S. Supreme Court therefore had ruled that defendants violating that law could not be required, consistent with the Eighth Amendment, to forfeit large amounts of money since the crime was merely a reporting offense. The criminal offense of bulk cash smuggling is designed to remedy this ruling. Prosecutors have used section 371 of the USA PATRIOT Act to obtain the forfeiture of millions of dollars connected with terrorism and drug dealers.

Decreasing Terrorist Prosperity

The Patriot Act dramatically increased our ability to choke off terrorist monies, without which [terrorists] are rendered utterly ineffective. Renewal of the Act is one of the most important steps we can take to defeat the killers, to force them back into their tunnels and holes, starved of the resources it would take to build a bomb, pilot a plane or harness a virus.

A decrease in terrorist prosperity will lead to an increase in American prosperity. Because when we are confident in our safety and less prone to horrific attacks, we are freer to be creative, innovative, and productive. And the ability to do those things is what makes the American economy so special, so great.

John Snow, prepared remarks of Treasury Secretary Snow at Nanofilm in Cleveland, Ohio, July 13, 2004.

Alaa Al-Sadawi, a New Jersey imam with ties to a designated foreign terrorist organization, was charged with and convicted of violating section 371. Al-Sadawi had enlisted the help of his elderly parents in attempting to smuggle $659,000 in cash to Egypt. Specifically, customs agents discovered the currency in a box of Ritz crackers, two boxes of baby wipes, and a box of Quaker Oats inside a suitcase carried by his father on a commercial flight. Previously, this conduct could only have been prosecuted as a reporting offense, and prosecutors would not have been able to obtain forfeiture of all the unreported currency. Because of section

371 of the USA PATRIOT Act, however, the United States is currently seeking forfeiture of the entire $659,000 that Al-Sadawi was attempting to smuggle out of the country.

Bolstering Federal Law

In addition to allowing the federal government to obtain greater forfeitures from cash smugglers, section 806 of the USA PATRIOT Act bolstered federal law by expressly making terrorists' property subject to forfeiture. Specifically, the provision authorizes the government to seize property belonging to an individual or entity that plans or engages in domestic or international terrorism against the United States, acquired for use in future terrorist attacks, or representing the fruits of an act of terrorism. Prosecutors in Oregon recently used this provision to seize the assets of three defendants in the case of the Portland, Oregon terror cell discussed above.

Beyond making more assets subject to forfeiture, Congress also provided the Department in the USA PATRIOT Act with a new tool to seize those assets subject to forfeiture under 18 U.S.C. § 981 or under the Controlled Substances Act. Such assets include both terrorism-related assets and various other assets connected with illegal activity. Section 319 authorizes the government to seize funds subject to forfeiture that are located in a foreign bank account by authorizing the seizure of foreign banks' funds that are held in a correspondent U.S. account. This is true regardless of whether the money in the correspondent account is directly traceable to the money held in the foreign bank account. The Department has used section 319 in several significant cases.

On January 18, 2001, a federal grand jury indicted James Gibson for offenses including conspiracy to commit money laundering and mail and wire fraud. Gibson had defrauded his clients, who were numerous personal injury victims including widows, orphans, and those in need of expensive medical care, of millions of dollars by fraudulently structuring settlements. Gibson and his wife, who was indicted later, fled to Belize, depositing some of the proceeds from their scheme in two Belizean banks. The Department's efforts to recover the proceeds initially proved unsuccessful. Although

Belize's government initially agreed to freeze the money, a Belizean court lifted the freeze and prohibited the government from further assisting American law enforcement agencies. Efforts to break the impasse failed, while the Gibsons systematically drained their accounts in Belize by purchasing luxury items. Following the passage of the USA PATRIOT Act, a seizure warrant was served on the Belizean bank's correspondent account in the United States pursuant to section 319, and the remaining funds were recovered. The government intends to return the recovered $1.7 million to the victims of Gibson's fraud scheme.

| "Experts say there's no reason to believe the new financial surveillance measures will stop the next attack." |

The Patriot Act Does Not Reduce Terrorist Financing

John Berlau

In the following viewpoint John Berlau argues that the massive paperwork generated by the financial disclosure provisions of the Patriot Act swamps law enforcement with irrelevant information. The Patriot Act expands the financial surveillance power granted to law enforcement by the Bank Secrecy Act (BSA) of 1970. The volume of data was already difficult to make sense of, claims Berlau, and did not prevent the terrorist attacks of September 11, 2001. The BSA experience suggests that Patriot Act financial provisions will not prevent terrorist attacks but simply flood law enforcement with more useless data. Berlau is a staff writer for *Insight*, a national news magazine.

As you read, consider the following questions:
1. According to Berlau, what is the ratio between transaction reports banks file on innocent customers and money laundering convictions?
2. In the author's opinion, how did FinCEN contribute to the intelligence failure prior to the terrorist attacks of September 11, 2001?
3. What have been the costs of the 30-year experiment with the Bank Secrecy Act, in the author's view?

"This is really a bill which, if enacted into law, will be [a longer] step in the direction of stopping terrorism than any other we have had before this Congress in a long time," one of the bill's sponsors declared. The legislation authorized broad surveillance of financial transactions, bypassing the Fourth Amendment's normal protections against "unreasonable searches and seizures" by requiring businesses to collect and share information with the government. After the measure passed and was signed into law, the debate was far from over. The American Civil Liberties Union [ACLU] and other critics continued to rail against the law as an unnecessary breach of privacy.

"Under the act and regulations the reports go forward to the investigative or prosecuting agency . . . without notice to the customer," one civil libertarian wrote. "Delivery of the records without the requisite hearing of probable cause breaches the Fourth Amendment. . . . I am not yet ready to agree that America is so possessed with evil that we must level all constitutional barriers to give our civil authorities the tools to catch terrorists."

But times have changed, one of the law's defenders countered. "While an act conferring such broad authority over transactions such as these might well surprise or even shock those who lived in an earlier era," he wrote, "the latter did not . . . live to see the heavy utilization of our domestic banking system by the minions of organized terrorism as well as by millions of legitimate businessmen." The author did not "think it was strange or irrational that Congress, having its attention called to what appeared to be serious and organized efforts to avoid detection of terrorist activity, should have legislated to rectify the situation."

An Historical Debate

These may sound like the arguments for and against the USA PATRIOT Act, passed immediately after the [terrorist] attacks of September 11, 2001. But they concern another piece of legislation, the Bank Secrecy Act (BSA) of 1970. The only change I made to these decades-old quotes was to substitute the word terrorist for criminal and terrorism for crime.

The congressman was Wright Patman, the populist Texas

Democrat who pushed through the bill on the premise that it would help fight drug trafficking, tax evasion, and other crimes, including the then-prohibited ownership of gold—as a commodity. The civil libertarian was Supreme Court Justice William O. Douglas. In the 1974 case *California Bankers Association v. Schultz*, Douglas wrote a dissent, joined by Justices William Brennan and Thurgood Marshall, concluding that the Bank Secrecy Act violated the Fourth Amendment. The final quote is from William Rehnquist, now the Court's chief justice, who wrote the majority opinion upholding the law.

A Needle in a Haystack

The reason the arguments sound familiar is that the BSA set the precedent for much of the PATRIOT Act, not to mention government fishing expeditions such as the Pentagon's aborted Total Information Awareness program.[1] The law authorized the government to require bank reports of all transactions over a dollar value set by the Treasury Department, even if there is no reason to suspect a criminal connection. For the first time, in the words of the U.S. District Court for the Northern District of California, "the government claim[ed] the legal right to maintain routine surveillance, without summons, subpoena, or warrant, over the details of citizens' financial transactions."

The district court struck down the BSA's reporting requirement, but its decision was reversed by the Supreme Court. In a complicated majority opinion, Rehnquist said that banks, as businesses, don't have the same Fourth Amendment rights as individuals. The opinion relied on the many post–New Deal cases that minimized economic liberties, including one that said "corporations can claim no equality with individuals in the enjoyment of a right to privacy" In this and in a subsequent BSA case, *U.S. v. Miller* (1976), the Court ruled that a bank's customers generally lack standing to challenge the law.

Law enforcement agencies thus found a convenient end

---

1. The program hoped to design a vast surveillance database to track terror suspects. Some believed it would give government the power to generate a comprehensive data profile on any U.S. citizen.

run around the Fourth Amendment. They can access the details of a bank customer's transactions from the Treasury Department's Financial Crimes Enforcement Network (FinCEN) without showing probable cause—or any evidence at all. That is why the PATRIOT Act's defenders argue that the law is not a radical departure from what the government already had the power to do. Writing in the Summer 2003 issue of *City Journal,* the Manhattan institute's Heather Mac Donald accuses the PATRIOT Act's opponents of trying to "invent new rights," because it has long been the case that "there is no Fourth Amendment privacy right in records or other items disclosed to third parties."

A Poor Record Against Terrorism

While Mac Donald may be partly right about the case law, she overlooks two important questions. One is whether surveillance programs like FinCEN are consistent with the principles of a free society. The other is how effective they've been: Have we gotten more security during the last 30 years in exchange for the privacy we've sacrificed? Looking specifically at the BSA and other bank surveillance measures, prominent experts in law enforcement, national security, and technology say the answer is no. The record of FinCEN, the agency that was charged with tracking terrorist financing prior to 9/11, seems to vindicate their arguments. The lack of success with the financial information that the government has long been collecting does not bode well for more-ambitious data dredging plans. Indeed, experience suggests that piling up more data could make it harder to zero in on terrorists.

"I consider all these measures to be highly counterproductive," says John Yoder, director of the Justice Department's Asset Forfeiture Office in the Reagan administration. "It costs more to enforce and regulate them than the benefits that are received. You're getting so much data on people who are absolutely legitimate and who are doing nothing wrong. There's just so much paperwork out there that it's really not a targeted effort. You have investigators running around chasing innocent people, trying to find something that they're doing wrong, rather than targeting real criminals."

The Problem of Information Overload

The paperwork is indeed massive. Even before the PA-TRIOT Act, banks sent more than 12 million transaction reports to the government in 2000 alone. In a 2000 report for the Competitive Enterprise Institute, economist Lawrence Lindsey, who later became head of the Bush administration's National Economic Council, calculated that banks file more than 100,000 reports on innocent customers for every money laundering conviction. Oliver "Buck" Revell, a highly decorated 30-year veteran of the FBI who supervised the bureau's counterterrorism division in the 1980s and '90s, agrees that the sheer volume of data generated by these measures can overwhelm law enforcement efforts. "You can be buried in an avalanche of information," Revell says. "The total volume of activity makes it very difficult to track and trace any type of specific information. . . . It's virtually impossible to look at millions and millions of CTRs [currency transaction reports] and make any sense out of them if you don't have some prior intelligence as to what might be occurring."

Drowning in Dirty Money

After Congress rushed to pass the USA Patriot Act in the aftermath of [the September 11, 2001, terrorist attacks] terrorists, druglords, and other criminals continue to launder funds through U.S. financial institutions. Hundreds of billions more in illicit cash gushed through banks, brokerage firms, and the like . . . even though they are spending more than $11 billion to bolster their internal controls. . . .

The law is still hugely controversial. Civil libertarians argue that it infringes on people's privacy by giving law-enforcement agencies more power to get customer information from banks. It's a small price to pay if it succeeds, goes the counterargument. But what's becoming clear is that a major national priority to starve terrorists and others of dirty money—the September 11 hijackers used U.S. banks to transfer funds—is, in fact, failing.

Mara Der Hovanesian, *Business Week*, December 1, 2003.

Yoder argues that the information overload from bank surveillance contributed to the intelligence failure before the September 11 attacks. "We already had so much information that we weren't really focusing on the right stuff," he says. "What good does it do to gather more paperwork when you're already so awash in paperwork that you're not paying attention to your own currently existing intelligence gathering system?"

While it did not cite the BSA directly, the . . . joint Congressional inquiry report on intelligence lapses before 9/11 did find that law enforcement and intelligence agencies faced a "huge volume of intelligence reporting," within which were "various threads and pieces of information that, at least in retrospect, are relevant and significant." The report concluded that "although relevant information . . . was available to the intelligence Community prior to September 11, 2001, the Community too often failed to focus on that information and consider and appreciate its collective significance in terms of a probable terrorist attack." This was partly because analysts were trying to find a needle in a very large haystack of data created by laws like the BSA. . . .

The Citizen-Soldier Burden

Customer surveillance is not just at banks anymore. In his dissent in the California Bankers Association case, Justice Douglas made a sarcastic suggestion that turned out to be prophetic: "It would be highly useful to government espionage to have reports from all our bookstores, all our hardware and retail stores, all our drugstores. . . . What one buys at the hardware and retail stores may furnish clues to potential uses of wires, soap powders, and the like used by criminals."

Even before 9/11, FinCEN had put out a rule applying the "suspicious activity" reporting requirement to any establishment that processed money orders or sold smart cards, including convenience stores. The PATRIOT Act extended the requirement to many more businesses. FinCEN, pursuant to the act, recently put the "suspicious activity" reporting rules into effect for brokerage houses, and real estate transactions are next on the list. The law also specifically covers casinos, credit card agencies, and life insurers. . . . The *Broward Daily Business Review* reports, "the Treasury Department will decide whether the act covers travel agents, automobile dealers, mutual funds and dealers in precious metals and stones." And under the law, virtually all businesses, including the "hardware and retail stores" mentioned by Douglas, now have to report to the government any cash purchases over $10,000.

Treasury Department General Counsel David Aufhauser explained the new reporting requirements this way in a 2002 interview with *The Washington Post:* "The Patriot Act is imposing a citizen-soldier burden on the gatekeepers of financial institutions." He justified this burden by arguing that "they are in the best position to police attempts by people who would do ill to us in the U.S. to penetrate the financial system."

Surprising Supporters and Opponents

Few politicians, even among those who have criticized other parts of the PATRIOT Act, are willing to challenge the proposition that businesses should be deputized to spy on their customers. The late justices Douglas, Brennan, and Marshall might be shocked that liberal Democrats in Congress such as Sens. Carl Levin of Michigan and Paul Sarbanes of Maryland have been the biggest proponents of expanding the Bank Secrecy Act. They see it as a way of targeting wealthy people who pay less than their "fair share" in taxes by moving some of their investments overseas. The only member of Congress who has gone on record in support of repealing the BSA entirely is Rep. Ron Paul (R-Texas).

Yet given the BSA's track record, experts say there's no reason to believe the new financial surveillance measures will stop the next attack. They could simply swamp law enforcement with even more useless data. The critics say reporting mandates have flooded the government with massive volumes of irrelevant information, such as reports on the "suspicious activities" of law-abiding customers withdrawing large amounts of money for medical treatment or depositing thousands of dollars in casino winnings, and have not been effective in either attacking the drug trade or preventing terrorist attacks.

J. Michael Walter, vice president of the Center for Security Policy, a hawkish D.C. think tank, is usually not in sync with the ACLU. He fully supports Attorney General John

Ashcroft's detention of Arab visitors and advocates targeted ethnic profiling. But he calls the BSA's routine mass surveillance measures "really, really dumb.". . .

The Hawala Bungle

Although it was not one of the agencies covered in the 9/11 report, FinCEN had its own intelligence failures, and they cast light on how effective the expanded financial reporting mandates might be. In the months prior to 9/11, FinCEN appeared to be choking on the flood of bank reports it received. In the March 25, 2002, issue of *Insight*, Jamie Dettmer reported that "Treasury sources say there is a two-year backlog of SARs [suspicious activity reports] still waiting to be entered into the agency's computers." In addition, several banking compliance officers told him "they were unaware of any SARS they'd filed being followed up by federal investigators."

FinCEN apparently was so busy processing paperwork that it ignored the valuable advice of one of its experts—advice that many say could have led to the Al Qaeda [terrorist group] money trail. Patrick Jost, who came to FinCEN in the '90s with an atypical background as a jazz musician, linguistics instructor, and video game programmer, was an expert on hawala, the shadowy, informal system of money trading in South Asian and Middle Eastern countries that leaves a very faint paper trail. In a hawala transaction, someone from Pakistan living in America could send money back home by paying a U.S. vendor, who in turn would contact a trusted partner in Pakistan, who would give the money in local currency to its intended recipient. The money technically never leaves the U.S. It is a money transfer without money movement. Although hawala is often used for innocent purposes such as sending money to relatives, in the late '90s there was already evidence that it was being used by terrorists. As Jost documented in a 1998 paper he co-wrote for Interpol, terrorists used hawala to finance a series of bomb blasts in Bombay, India, in 1993.

William Wechsler, head of a White House working group on terrorist financing, met with Jost in 1999. Wechsler recalls that after hearing Jost's explanation of hawala, he spread the word to counterterrorism experts in the government, many of whom contacted Jost for help. Jost was also doing research on other aspects of terrorist financing, such as the countries terrorist money flows through. But FinCEN, even though it was charged with helping law enforcement track criminal money laundering, instructed him to decline Jost's offer of assistance and discouraged him from pursuing further research on terrorism financing. Jost told *The Washington Post* in 2001 that FinCEN Director James Sloan and Chief of Operations Connie Fenchel "didn't want FinCEN to pursue this line of work.' According to the *Post*, after being "made to feel unwelcome, Jost left government in June 2000."

Wechsler recalls that the issue of terrorism did not seem to be a high priority for FinCEN, which appeared much more interested in processing data for the drug war. "FinCEN, along with the rest of the federal law enforcement community, for too long assigned far too low a priority to understanding the nature of and the threat from underground remittance systems, like the hawala network," he says.

Now that supposedly has changed. FinCEN has set up a toll-free number for banks to report transactions they truly think are suspicious, and the Treasury Department has a targeted "watch list" of suspected terrorists for banks to report on. But FinCEN and other agencies will still be inundated with an even bigger flood of reports about mostly legal financial transactions, thanks to the mandates of the BSA and the PATRIOT Act.

Wechsler, along with other Clinton administration officials such as Treasury Undersecretary Stuart Eizenstat, supported the expansion of "suspicious activity" reporting. (He proudly claims that "there are a lot of provisions of the PATRIOT Act that the Clinton administration had asked for.") He argues that new technology will be able to sift through the data. "We should spend the money that it takes to make sure we are able to use the information as effectively as possible, and that we are able to give back to the banking community the after-action reports, how it was used," he says. "But all of those are marginal questions compared to the overall statement that this is way too burdensome and useless. It's nonsense; it's very useful."

Yet for 30 years agencies have said technology eventually

would be able to pinpoint the needle in this enormous haystack, and the elusive technology has yet to appear. The Pentagon's Total Information Awareness (TIA) project was aimed at developing methods to sift through huge volumes of data from public and private sources, looking for patterns that could indicate terrorist activity. After a loud public outcry about the privacy implications, Congress voted . . . to deny the project funding. . . .

Thirty Years of Failure

"When you are scanning a population that is composed of hundreds of millions of people, and the class of criminal you're looking for is a couple hundred or a couple thousand, there are no tools available, and there are almost certainly never going to be tools available, with the sophistication to focus almost exclusively on the bad guys," says Bob Gellman, who in the '90s acted as chief counsel of a House subcommittee on privacy and technology. Gellman says data mining's success in the private sector will never translate to law enforcement because a different level of precision is required. "If direct marketing companies, with all the research they do, get a 3 percent response rate, they're ecstatic," Gellman says. "And these are smart people with lots of data and lots of motivation because they're making money, and they can't do much better than that."

In the debate over the PATRIOT Act and other broad surveillance measures, the Bank Secrecy Act should be thought of as a 30-year experiment in subverting the Fourth Amendment. The experiment has imposed tremendous costs on individual privacy and the economy (even before 9/11, the banking industry was estimating compliance costs of $10 billion a year), with few tangible results in stopping crime and even fewer in preventing terrorism. Getting back to the standards of the Fourth Amendment is a good idea, not just for securing privacy but for making law enforcement and intelligence agencies more focused and effective at stopping criminals and catching terrorists.

"Most police officers, I find, have very high regard for and deference to the Fourth Amendment," says Bob Barr, the former CIA agent and U.S. attorney who served as a Republican congressman from Georgia for eight years and is now a consultant on privacy issues for the ACLU and the American Conservative Union. "I think they understand, perhaps better than a lot of bigwigs, that it is there to protect them and to help keep them focused as well as to protect the individuals."

Periodical Bibliography

The following articles have been selected to supplement the diverse views presented in this chapter.

Doug Bandow
"Protecting Security in a Nation of Laws," *Conservative Chronicle*, August 20, 2003.

John Berlau
"Money Laundering and Mission Creep: The Costly and Intrusive Money-Laundering Provisions Put into the USA PATRIOT Act at the Insistence of Democrats Are in Use for More than Terrorism Cases," *Insight*, January 5, 2004.

David Freddoso
"Patriot Act Aided in 179 Terror Convictions," *Human Events*, July 19, 2004.

Nat Hentoff
"Bush-Ashcroft vs. Homeland Security," *Village Voice*, April 23–29, 2003.

William F. Jasper
"Trading Freedom for Security," *New American*, May 5, 2003.

Rosemary Jenks
"The USA PATRIOT Act of 2001: A Summary of the Anti-Terrorism Law's Immigration-Related Provisions," *Center for Immigration Studies Backgrounder*, December 2001.

Martin Kady
"Homeland Security," *CQ Researcher*, September 12, 2003.

Anthony Lewis
"Un-American Activities," *New York Review of Books*, October 23, 2003.

Rich Lowry
"Patriot Hysteria," *National Review*, August 28, 2003.

Heather Mac Donald
"Straight Talk on Homeland Security," *City Journal*, Summer 2003.

Bill McIntyre
"Crush the Terrorists . . . Not the Bill of Rights," *Shield*, Spring 2002.

Hudson Morgan
"Laundry Bag—Treasury's Kid Gloves," *New Republic*, April 14, 2004.

Kelly Patricia O'Meara
"Police State," *Insight*, December 3, 2001.

Richard W. Rahn and Veronique de Rugy
"Threats to Financial Privacy and Tax Competition," *Policy Analysis*, October 2, 2004.

Anita Ramasastry
"Indefinite Detention Based upon Suspicion: How the Patriot Act Will Disrupt Many Lawful Immigrants' Lives," *FindLaw's Writ*, October 5, 2001.

Does the Patriot Act Violate Civil Liberties?

Chapter Preface

From the time the Patriot Act was signed into law on October 26, 2001, supporters and critics have debated its utility and its constitutionality. Supporters claim that the act helps fight terrorism, citing successful terrorist prosecutions. Critics claim that the act violates the civil liberties of law-abiding citizens without their knowledge. Because information obtained by the Justice Department is classified by the act, however, critics cannot prove their claims. According to journalist Amy Goldstein, "The paradox of this debate is that it is playing out in a near-total information vacuum: By its very terms, the Patriot Act hides information about how its most contentious aspects are used, allowing investigations to be authorized and conducted under greater secrecy." Critics claim that such secrecy prevents the congressional oversight necessary to protect civil liberties. The Justice Department, on the other hand, contends that national security necessitates that the information sought remain classified.

In 2002 the House and Senate Judiciary committees, which are responsible for overseeing the Justice Department, began to send requests to the department, asking that Attorney General John Ashcroft provide details about how often and in what way Patriot Act provisions had been used. One letter asked that Ashcroft provide specific details about how the department, specifically the FBI, was using wiretaps, surveillance, and secret searches. The Justice Department released a report that provided little information, claiming that the information sought by lawmakers was classified. According to Goldstein, "One document was a six-page list of instances in which 'national security letters' had been issued to authorize searches—with every line blacked out."

Critics of the Patriot Act contend that the Justice Department's reluctance to disclose more about the act's use impedes congressional oversight. Such oversight is impossible, these analysts argue, without sufficient detail about how the Justice Department and its enforcement agencies such as the FBI are implementing the act's provisions. "The problem is, we don't know how [the act] has been used," claims law professor David Cole, who represents terror suspects in cases in which the government has employed secret evidence.

The Justice Department disputes such claims, maintaining that it has cooperated fully with the House and Senate Judiciary committees. The Justice Department contends, "Since the attacks of September 11th, the Department of Justice has provided witnesses for 115 hearings before Congress related to the Patriot Act and the ongoing war against terrorism. The Department has also provided over 100 pages of responses to House Judiciary Committee questions on the Department's implementation of the Patriot Act." Some oversight committee members agree. After receiving the Justice Department's response to a May 2003 request for information, House Judiciary Committee chairman Jim Sensenbrenner claims, "The Justice Department should be commended for the timing and thoroughness of these answers. These answers will assist the Judiciary Committee in fulfilling its legislative and oversight responsibilities and should prove helpful in any future debate about extending all or part of the USA PATRIOT Act."

Whether or not the information provided by the Justice Department is sufficient to ensure that civil liberties are being protected remains controversial. The authors in the following chapter debate whether or not the Patriot Act—especially its provisions pertaining to surveillance and secrecy—threatens America's civil liberties.

*"The USA PATRIOT Act is one of the
most sweeping acts in modern American
history because of its potential impact on
. . . civil liberties."*

The Patriot Act Violates Civil Liberties

Jim Cornehls

The Patriot Act threatens civil liberties in numerous ways, argues Jim Cornehls in the following viewpoint. Passed in the wake of the terrorist attacks of September 11, 2001, the complex, 342-page act defines terrorism so broadly that it encompasses constitutionally protected acts of civil disobedience, claims Cornehls. With little or no oversight, he contends, the act grants broad police powers that sidestep constitutional controls on the surveillance, arrest, and prosecution of American citizens. Cornehls is a professor and director of the Law and Public Policy Graduate Certificate Program in the School of Urban and Public Affairs, University of Texas at Arlington.

As you read, consider the following questions:

1. According to Cornehls, the Patriot Act's broad definition of terrorism might encompass the activities of what organizations?
2. What must the government assert in order for the courts to issue warrants and orders under the Patriot Act, in the author's view?
3. In the author's opinion, what is different about the Patriot Act's restrictions and earlier restrictions on civil rights?

Jim Cornehls, "The USA PATRIOT Act: The Assault on Civil Liberties," Z *Magazine*, vol. 16, July 2003. Copyright © 2003 by Jim Cornehls. Reproduced by permission.

September 11, 2001, marked a momentous and tragic event in U.S. history. It also evoked a flood of patriotic fervor and an instant fear that Americans now were vulnerable to international terrorism. Capitalizing on these fears, the executive and legislative branches of the U.S. government quickly enacted measures purported to counteract terrorism or terrorist threats. One of the principal results of this activity was an act titled "Uniting and Strengthening America by Providing Appropriate Tools Required to Intercept and Obstruct Terrorism Act of 2001," or, the USA PATRIOT Act, passed and signed into law by President [George W.] Bush on October 26, 2001. The USA PATRIOT Act is one of the most sweeping acts in modern American history because of its potential impact on the civil liberties of U.S. citizens and non-U.S. citizens residing in the United States.

A Complex Law

It is hard to believe the Act could have been drafted, debated, and passed in only 45 days. It is over 342 pages long and extremely complicated. Given its complexity, and the fact the legislation represented a wish list of new investigative and detention powers long sought by law enforcement officials, it is more likely the pro-law enforcement Administration had been drafting such provisions for many months. Post-September 11 provided the perfect opportunity to introduce them, with very little Congressional or public opposition. The Senate voted for the Act 98 to 1 and the House 356 to 66. The vast majority of Americans never even heard of it at the time.

The Act is complex and difficult to grasp because of its multiple references to and incorporation of other foreign intelligence acts, principally the Foreign Intelligence Surveillance Act (FISA). Congressional hearings were minimal and the legislation was not accompanied by either a committee or conference report. Nonetheless, in the meager hearings that took place, the Act was vigorously opposed by numerous civil rights groups, especially the Center for Constitutional Rights (CCR) and the American Civil Liberties Union (ACLU), who warned that the Act was constitutionally defective and represented a broad attack on many of the traditional civil liberties enjoyed in the U.S.

A Broad Definition of Terrorism

One of the most significant features of the Act is a new, broader definition given to terrorism. The definition now also includes "domestic," as contrasted with international terrorism. Section 802 states that a person engages in domestic terrorism if they do any act "dangerous to human life" that is a violation of the criminal laws of a state or the United States, if that action appears to be intended to: (i) intimidate or coerce a civilian population; (ii) influence the policy of a government by intimidation or coercion; or (iii) to affect the conduct of a government by mass destruction, assassination, or kidnapping. Further, the act or acts must take place primarily within the territorial jurisdiction of the United States.

This definition is broad enough to encompass the activities of such organizations as Greenpeace, Operation Rescue Environmental Liberation Front, protests about Vieques Island,[1] and protests at the meeting of the World Trade Organization. Civil disobedience, such as entering on the premises of a U.S. military base, which is a violation of federal law, would now be included within the definition of an act of domestic terrorism. Disrupting a meeting or procession of vehicles as a means of drawing attention to or attempting to influence an unwanted governmental policy all could be considered acts of domestic terrorism. The implications are huge and the Act can be used to prosecute political dissidents of many stripes. The Act potentially violates at least six of the ten original Bill of Rights: the 1st, 4th, 5th, 6th, 7th, 8th, and 13th Amendment. It grants broad new powers to law enforcement and permits law enforcement officials to sidestep or avoid entirely many traditional controls on the surveillance, investigation, arrest, and prosecution of civilians residing in the United States.

1. In February 2000 tens of thousands of people, organized by church leaders, gathered in Puerto Rico, calling on the United States not to resume military exercises on the neighboring island of Vieques.

The first effects of the Act were soon felt when the government secretly arrested and jailed more than 1,200 people in connection with its investigation of the events of September 11. Despite demands from members of Congress, numerous civil liberties and human rights organizations, and the media, the Government refused to make public the number of people arrested, their names, their lawyers, the reasons for their arrest, and other information related to their whereabouts and circumstances.

Challenging the PATRIOT Act

After first failing, by means of the Freedom of Information Act (FOIA), to obtain information about those arrested and held, multiple organizations joined to file suit in federal district court in Washington, DC (*Center for National Security Studies, et al. v. U.S. Department of Justice*). The government still refused to provide the requested information, citing several exemptions under FOIA. A final order in the case was not entered until August 2, 2002, which required the government to divulge the names of almost all those arrested. By that time most of those arrested had been either released or deported.

Many of those arrested and jailed were Arabs and Muslims, who were cab drivers, construction workers, and other laborers, with no more than ordinary visa violations. Many of them were caught up in routine traffic stops and other incidental contacts with law enforcement officials. Some were incarcerated for up to seven months without being charged or permitted to see their families. Despite the lower court's ruling, the government still refused to divulge the names of those arrested and is appealing the decision.

In a related secrecy issue, the American Civil Liberties Union, the National Association of Criminal Defense Lawyers, and others sought to have the Supreme Court review a secret appeals court decision that broadly expanded the government's power to spy on U.S. citizens. The special, secret court was created in 1978 with the passage of the Foreign Intelligence Surveillance Act. Its purpose was to review and approve government wiretaps in foreign intelligence investigations. All hearings and decisions of the court are conducted in secret. Now, under the PATRIOT Act's new definition of foreign intelligence investigations, its role is being expanded to include domestic investigations that the government claims are related to foreign intelligence. The Supreme Court, in its first decision on an issue related to the PATRIOT Act, refused the request to review the secret decision of this special court.

Kirk. © 2004 by Kirk Anderson. Reproduced by permission.

In subsequent months, the PATRIOT Act was challenged on other grounds. The Justice Department used the Act to declare two American citizens enemy combatants. They then were held as military prisoners, denied the right to an attorney or access to civilian courts, and left without a roadmap as to how they could challenge their imprisonment. One was arrested in Afghanistan, the other in Chicago. The Justice Department took the position that it was improper for courts to inquire too deeply into the government's classification of a U.S. citizen as an enemy combatant. The District Court in Norfolk, Virginia ruled that the two-page memo provided by the government to explain its decision in one of these instances was inadequate. However, that ruling was overturned by a three-judge panel of the Fourth Circuit in Richmond in January 2003. On March 11, [2002] Manhattan U.S. District Judge Michael Mukasey stood by his earlier, December ruling to allow one of the U.S. citizens, Jose Padilla, who was arrested in Chicago, to meet with defense lawyers. The Justice Department announced it would study the opinion before deciding whether to appeal.

Another area in which the Act has been challenged concerns the Administration's decision to hold as many as 600 deportation hearings in secret. It did this based on the Attorney General's assertion that those detained for deportation were suspected of having links to terrorism. A federal district judge in New Jersey ordered that all such deportation hearings be opened to the public unless the government could show, on a case-by-case basis, there was a need for secrecy. That decision also was overturned, by the Third Circuit Court of Appeals in Philadelphia, which held that secrecy was warranted by the grave threats to the nation.

Meanwhile, the Sixth Circuit Court of Appeals in Cincinnati upheld a lower court decision that such deportation hearings must be open, unless good cause is shown for secrecy. That is now the law in Kentucky, Michigan, Ohio, and Tennessee and makes it likely the Supreme Court will consider at least one of these cases to resolve the conflict. However, since most deportation hearings are heard in New Jersey, the Cincinnati court's ruling may be little more than a gesture.

All told, through mid-March, 2003, the ACLU had filed or participated as a plaintiff in 31 lawsuits and friend of the court briefs in connection with government activities involving arrest, detention, surveillance, and First Amendment violations, in which countering possible terrorist acts was the ostensible reason for the actions. The number of other government violations of civil liberties that have gone unchallenged is inestimable.

Aside from these court challenges, the PATRIOT Act insinuated itself into the everyday lives of ordinary Americans in a variety of ways. While the PATRIOT Act granted extensive new powers to law enforcement, the Bush administration augmented and extended these powers through the issuance of 11 new executive orders, 10 new interim agency regulations, and 2 final regulations implemented by the Justice Department. In this way the Administration sidestepped both the legislative and judicial branches. Government investigations pursuant to the Act are shrouded in secrecy, such as the closed deportation hearings, the secret arrests, and the new power of the government to enter and search the homes of private citizens without notifying them.

Suppressing Press Speech

Yet another government power under the Act requires courts to issue warrants and orders based on the mere government assertion that the order is sought in connection with a terrorism investigation. These warrants and orders permit the FBI to question any person about coworkers and other persons and to demand access to records about such individuals. The Court order also warns the person questioned not to reveal anything about the contact to anyone else, under threat of criminal sanctions. As a result, it is difficult to determine just what law enforcement officials using the Act are actually doing. The chilling effect of the Act on free speech and political dissent has been felt already. Individuals have been questioned by the FBI about their political beliefs for being openly critical of a possible war against Iraq. In San Francisco, a 60-year-old retiree remarked at his local gym that he thought any war with Iraq was not just about fighting terrorists, but about corporate profits and oil. He promptly received a visit at home from the FBI with questions about his political beliefs.

The FBI paid a call on a North Carolina college student for displaying an "un-American poster" in her own home. The poster in question was critical of President Bush's stand on capital punishment while serving as governor of Texas. . . .

Federal agents spent an hour or more inspecting a car museum in Houston, Texas based on a tip that artwork on display at the museum was "of a nature threatening to the president." There were no such artworks, but the agents questioned a museum docent about the artists, who funded the museum, and who had visited the exhibit.

Other low ranking quasi-law enforcement officials have eagerly joined in the suppression of individual First Amendment rights since the passage of the Act. Recently, in a shopping mall in Guilderland, New York, a 61-year-old lawyer and his son were wearing T-shirts that read "Peace On Earth" and "Give Peace A Chance." They were ordered by mall security guards to remove the offending shirts or leave the mall. The lawyer refused and was charged with trespassing. . . . Natalie Maines, the lead singer for the Dixie Chicks, an all-female country and western group, spoke out in opposition to the Administration's war policies in Iraq and criticized President Bush. Subsequently, at a pro-war rally organized by radio station KRMD, part of a radio chain, which banned the Dixie Chicks from its play lists, a tractor was used to smash a collection of Dixie Chicks CDs, tapes, and other paraphernalia, while a supportive crowd looked on.

Other, pro-war Bush rallies were sponsored around the nation by radio stations. Called Rally for America, Clear Channel Communications organized them. Clear Channel is a San Antonio–based organization that controls more than 1,200 radio stations and whose vice chairperson, Tom Hicks, is a close friend and political supporter of President Bush.

Since September 11, there have been innumerable instances of public officials, quasi-public officials, and private citizens attempting to control political speech. These range from banning public rallies and peaceful marches to the cancellation of a Baseball Hall of Fame appearance by Tim Robbins, Susan Sarandon, and Dale Petroskey, the president of the Baseball Hall of Fame.

A History of Suppression

There were other instances in American history when the government adopted extraordinary measures to suppress unpopular political views or arrest those suspected of being disloyal to the United States. During the Civil War, President [Abraham] Lincoln suspended the writ of habeas corpus. As a result tens of thousands of Americans suspected of being disloyal to the Union were arrested and held without charges by the military. During World War I, and the Red Scare, as many as 10,000 resident aliens, targeted because of their political views, were arrested, interrogated, jailed, and beaten to force them to sign confessions. Raids were carried out in over 30 cities and some 500 "aliens" were deported. During World War II, President Roosevelt issued an executive order for the forced internment of 110,000 persons of Japanese ancestry living on the U.S. West Coast. Two-thirds of those placed in so-called preventive detention, under harsh conditions, were U.S. citizens against whom there was no evidence of collaboration with the Japanese.

During the Cold War, in the late 1940s and early 1950s, when fears of communism were fueled by certain U.S. political leaders and anti-Communist hysteria was rampant, leaders of the American Communist Party were criminally prosecuted and imprisoned under the Smith Act for their political beliefs. The House Un-American Activities Committee carried out a witch hunt of suspected Communists and so-called "fellow travelers." Thousands of Americans were subpoenaed and called to testify about their own and other Americans' political affiliations and activities. Those who refused to testify were held in contempt and imprisoned. In other instances, college professors and other employees were forced to sign so-called loyalty oaths or lose their jobs.

Richard Posner, a conservative federal jurist in Chicago, uses the above instances to argue that the current measures taken under the PATRIOT Act are not that worrisome. He urges the use of cost/benefit analysis to weigh the relative importance of liberty vs. security at a time of perceived threats to security. He believes that in time, when the threats to security have waned, a balance between liberty and security interests will be restored.

Expanding the PATRIOT Act

This sanguine view overlooks the fact that the earlier restrictions on civil rights were one-time phenomena, more specifically targeted, and narrow in scope. In the case of the PATRIOT Act, the restrictions are broad, indefinite, and far-reaching. The Administration insists the war on terrorism is open-ended and will continue for many years, if not indefinitely. Many of the emergency measures to combat the threat of terrorism will likely become permanent and even more comprehensive. Senator Orrin Hatch, a leading congressional supporter of the PATRIOT Act, recently tried quietly to introduce amendments to strengthen the Act and make it permanent.

Already, there is a new bill, prepared by the Justice Department, entitled the Domestic Security Enhancement Act of 2003. Dubbed PATRIOT II, the new act seeks to further expand the government's powers to combat suspected terrorism and further encroaches on civil liberties.[2] According to David Cole, a Georgetown University law professor, the proposed new act will expand the authority of law enforcement and intelligence gathering agencies; reduce or eliminate entirely judicial oversight of surveillance; permit wiretapping of Americans—without any court order—for 15 days if the executive branch decides there is a national emergency; authorize secret arrests; create a DNA data bank based solely on unconfirmed executive suspicion; create new offenses punishable with the death penalty; and seek to strip Americans of their citizenship if they belong to or support disfavored political groups. Perhaps as importantly, the draft bill was produced in secret, without consultation with Congress. Senior members of the Senate Judiciary Committee minority staff, who inquired of the Justice Department about any such proposed legislation, were informed that no such legislation was being planned only a few days before the proposed bill was publicly revealed on PBS's "Frontline NOW." The U.S. Attorney General, John Ashcroft, has swept aside all criticism of the Administration's current disregard for traditional civil liberties by publicly proclaiming that extraordinary times call for extraordinary measures. Ashcroft's views are so extreme that he has alarmed even the conservative right wing of the Republican Party. While agreeing with his position on abortion and child pornography, they are asking how they and their own organizations might fare under the new rules affecting civil liberties. If another power were to occupy the United States and institute the policies provided for in the USA PATRIOT Act—secret arrests, secret trials, secret investigations, secret deportations—the United States would be considered a police state.

The federal government is also enlisting American universities to assist in maintaining surveillance of foreign stu-

2. PATRIOT II has not been officially introduced in either house of Congress and has no official standing. Some claim, however, that portions of the drafted bill have been attached to other bills.

dents residing in the United States. The Student and Exchange Visitor Program (SEVIS), launched February 15, 2003, will involve almost 6,000 U.S. colleges and universities in gathering and forwarding information about foreign students to a national computer data bank. Along with other information gathered, the schools must notify the Immigration and Naturalization Service (INS) if a foreign student fails to enroll or is arrested. Institutions that do not have INS approval to participate in the data gathering system will be prohibited from enrolling new foreign students. (On March 1, 2003, the INS was merged into the new Department of Homeland Security and is now the Bureau of Citizenship and Immigration Services.)

[In February 2003] a Jordanian foreign exchange student, who confessed to once having had thoughts of being a terrorist martyr, but subsequently renounced those ideas, was summarily ordered deported within five days by a U.S. immigration judge in Dallas. The student, three months shy of earning a master's degree in software engineering at a Texas university, was under investigation by the FBI for undisclosed reasons.

Currently being put into effect is another new plan, dubbed CAPPS II, in cooperation with U.S. airlines. It will check the backgrounds of all commercial passengers and assign them a threat level of red, yellow, or green. Information about the passengers' credit reports, bank account activity, and cross checks with the names of persons on a government watch list were to be instituted by Delta Airlines about April 1, 2003. A comprehensive system that includes all airlines should be in place by the end of [2003].[1]

Creating comprehensive homeland security would cost trillions of dollars and completely change the way Americans lead their lives. It would include national identity cards, surveillance, and subject to search rules in all public places, random searches of vehicles entering airports and parking garages, compiling dossiers on all persons who take scuba diving lessons, tracking the comings and goings of subway riders electronically, and the list goes on and on. Virtually

1. As of January 2005, CAPPS II is still being tested.

everything anyone does, 24 hours a day, would be subject to constant surveillance.

Already, the security measures put in place in New York City are a portent of things to come throughout the nation. There is a proliferation of armed security guards, surveillance cameras, handbag searches, metal detectors, electronic access cards, and bomb sniffing dogs from the railroad terminals to the art museums. Heavily-armed police officers, dressed like assault troops, patrol landmark buildings such as St. Patrick's Cathedral in midtown Manhattan. The costs of these measures—and these are just the tip of the iceberg—are potentially astronomical. The costs in terms of the loss of civil liberties are incalculable.

As the scope of the Act and the threats it represents to all U.S. residents became more apparent, more than 100 municipalities and Hawaii, passed resolutions in opposition to the Act. Some encouraged public employees not to comply with the Act's most invasive and civil rights threatening features. One, Arcata, California, criminalized compliance with the Act. But the main features of a U.S. police state are already in place and it will take a major groundswell of public opposition to undo them.

"Most of the concerns about Patriot are misguided or based on premises that are just plain wrong."

Claims That the Patriot Act Violates Civil Liberties Are Unfounded

Ramesh Ponnuru

Claims that the Patriot Act violates civil liberties are flawed, claims Ramesh Ponnuru in the following viewpoint. Many of the act's provisions, he maintains, simply expand laws regulating criminal investigations to include terrorist investigations. For example, Ponnuru argues, the act extends the use of roving wiretaps, which have long been authorized for criminal cases, to terrorism investigations. Unfounded claims that the act violates civil liberties create unnecessary controversy and threaten to eliminate tools needed to fight terrorism, he asserts. Ponnuru comments on national politics and public policy issues on television, radio, and as senior editor of *National Review*.

As you read, consider the following questions:

1. What has resulted from the failure of the press to adequately scrutinize civil libertarians' claims about the Patriot Act, in the opinion of Ponnuru?
2. According to the author, what is the difference between Omnivore and Carnivore wiretaps?
3. What is the cost of legal laxity, in the author's view?

Ramesh Ponnuru, "1984 in 2003?: Fears About the Patriot Act Are Misguided," *National Review*, vol. 55, June 2, 2003. Copyright © 2003 by the National Review, Inc., 215 Lexington Ave., New York, NY 10016. Reproduced by permission.

Has the war on terrorism become a war on Americans' civil liberties? A coalition of left- and right-wing groups fears so, and has been working hard to restrain the law-and-order impulses of the Bush administration. It's a coalition that includes the ACLU [American Civil Liberties Union] and the American Conservative Union, [liberal columnist] Nat Hentoff and, [conservative columnist] William Safire, [liberal congressman] John Conyers and [conservative congressman] Dick Armey.

Restraining Anti-Terrorism Efforts

The coalition started to form in 1996, when Congress passed an anti-terrorism bill. But it really took off after [the terrorist attacks of] September 11 [2001]. Members of the coalition believe that Washington's legislative response—called, rather ludicrously, the "USA Patriot Act," an acronym for "Uniting and Strengthening America by Providing Appropriate Tools to Intercept and Obstruct Terrorism"—was a too-hastily conceived, excessive reaction to the atrocities.

Since then, the coalition has regularly found new cause for alarm. It has protested the administration's plans for military tribunals, the president's designation of "enemy combatants," and the Pentagon's attempts to consolidate data under a program called "Total Information Awareness." [In the spring of 2003] the civil libertarians of left and right worked together again to block Sen. Orrin Hatch's attempt to make permanent those provisions of the Patriot Act which are set to expire [in 2004]. They have organized, as well, against the possibility that the Justice Department will propose another dangerous anti-terror bill ("Patriot II").[1]

The civil libertarians have had some success. They forced modifications in the Patriot Act before its enactment. They have inspired some cities to pass resolutions banning their employees from cooperating with federal authorities to implement provisions of the act that violate the Constitution. (Officials in other cities are, presumably, free to violate the

1. Patriot II has not been officially introduced in either house of Congress and has no official standing. Some claim, however, that portions of the drafted bill have been attached to other bills.

Constitution at will.) They imposed legislative restrictions on Total Information Awareness.[2] They have inhibited the administration from proposing anti-terror measures that would generate adverse publicity.

The Role of the Press

They themselves have gotten favorable publicity. It's an irresistible story for the press: the lion and the lamb lying down together. The press has tended to marvel at the mere existence of the coalition. They have not been quick to note that there is a larger bipartisan coalition on the other side, which is why the civil libertarians have been losing most of the battles. The Patriot Act passed 357-66 in the House and 98-1 in the Senate. In early May [2003], the Senate voted 90-4 to approve another anti-terror provision—making it easier to investigate "lone wolf" terrorists with no proven connection to larger organizations—that the civil libertarians oppose.

More important, the press has not adequately scrutinized the civil libertarians' claims. This has kept the debate mired in platitudes about liberty and security. It has also reduced the incentive for the civil libertarians to do their homework, which has in turn made their case both weaker and more hysterical than it might otherwise have been.

Take the attack on TIPS, the Terrorist Information and Prevention System. This abortive plan would have encouraged trackers, deliverymen, and the like to report suspicious behavior they observed in the course of their work. How effective this idea would have been is open to question. Most of the criticism, however, echoed former Republican congressman Bob Barr, who said that TIPS "smacks of the very type of fascist or communist government we fought so hard to eradicate in other countries in decades past."

But of all the measures the administration has adopted, it's the Patriot Act (along with the possible Patriot II) that has inspired the most overheated criticisms. When it was passed, the Electronic Frontier Foundation wrote that "the civil lib-

2. The purpose of this program was to design a vast surveillance database to track terror suspects. Some believed it would give government the power to generate a comprehensive data profile on any U.S. citizen.

erties of ordinary Americans have taken a tremendous blow with this law." The ACLU says the law "gives the Executive Branch sweeping new powers that undermine the Bill of Rights." But most of the concerns about Patriot are misguided or based on premises that are just plain wrong.

Challenging the Critics

Roving wiretaps. Thanks to the Patriot Act, terrorism investigations can use roving wiretaps. Instead of having to get new judicial authorization for each phone number tapped, investigators can tap any phone their target uses. This is important when fighting terrorists whose MO [modus operandi] includes frequently switching hotel rooms and cell phones. It's a commonsense measure. It's also nothing new: Congress authorized roving wiretaps in ordinary criminal cases back in 1986. It's hard to see Patriot as a blow to civil liberties on this score.

Internet surveillance. Libertarians have been particularly exercised about Patriot's green light for "spying on the Web browsers of people who are not even criminal suspects"—to quote *Reason* editor Nick Gillespie. This is a misunderstanding of Patriot, as George Washington University law professor Orin Kerr has demonstrated in a law-review article. Before Patriot, it wasn't clear that any statute limited the government's, or even a private party's, ability to obtain basic information about electronic communications (e.g., to whom you're sending e-mails). Patriot required a court order to get that information, and made it a federal crime to get it without one.

Kerr believes that the bar for getting a court order should be raised. But he notes that Patriot made the privacy protections for the Internet as strong as those for phone calls and stronger than for mail. Patriot's Internet provisions, he concludes, "updated the surveillance laws without substantially shifting the balance between privacy and security."

James Bovard traffics in another Patriot myth in a recent cover story for *The American Conservative:* that it "empowers federal agents to cannibalize Americans' e-mail with Carnivore wiretaps." Carnivore is an Internet surveillance tool designed by the FBI. Don't be scared by the name. The FBI's previous tool was dubbed "Omnivore," and this new one was so-named because it would be more selective in acquiring information, getting only what was covered by a court order and leaving other information private. But even if Carnivore is a menace, it's not the fault of Patriot. As Kerr points out, "The only provisions of the Patriot Act that directly address Carnivore are pro-privacy provisions that actually restrict the use of Carnivore."

Hacking. Also in *Reason*, Jesse Walker writes that Patriot "expands the definition of terrorist to include such non-lethal acts as computer hacking." That's misleading. Pre-Patriot, an al-Qaeda [terrorist group] member who hacked the electric company's computers to take out the grid could not be judged guilty of terrorism, even if he would be so judged if he accomplished the same result with a bomb. Hacking per se isn't terrorism, and Patriot doesn't treat it as such.

The Support of the People

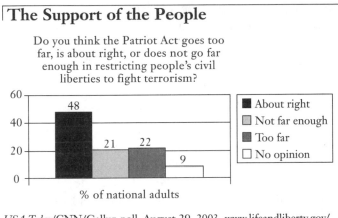

Do you think the Patriot Act goes too far, is about right, or does not go far enough in restricting people's civil liberties to fight terrorism?

■ About right
☐ Not far enough
■ Too far
☐ No opinion

% of national adults

USA Today/CNN/Gallup poll, August 29, 2003. www.lifeandliberty.gov/ subs/s_people.htm.

Sneak and peek. The ACLU is running ads that say that Patriot lets the government "secretly enter your home while you're away . . . rifle through your personal belongings . . . download your computer files . . . and seize any items at will." Worst of all, "you may never know what the government has done." Reality check: You will be notified if a sneak-and-peek search has been done, just after the fact—usually within a few days. The feds had the authority to conduct these searches before Patriot. A federal judge has to authorize such a search warrant, and the warrant has to specify what's to be seized.

Library records. Bovard is appalled that Patriot allows "federal agents to commandeer library records," and the American Library Association shares his sentiment. Patriot doesn't mention libraries specifically, but does authorize terrorism investigators to collect tangible records generally. Law enforcement has, however, traditionally been able to obtain library records with a subpoena. Prof. Kerr suggests that because of Patriot, the privacy of library records may be better protected in terrorism investigations than it is in ordinary criminal ones.

The civil libertarians deserve some credit. Their objections helped to rid Patriot of some provisions—such as a crackdown on Internet gambling—that didn't belong in an anti-terrorism bill. Armey added the Carnivore protections to the bill. The law, as finally enacted, places limits on how much officials may disclose of the information they gain from Internet and phone surveillance. Moreover, the civil libertarians make a reasonable demand when they ask that Patriot be subject to periodic re-authorizations, so that Congress can regularly consider making modifications.

The Cost of Restricting Intelligence

The civil libertarians rarely acknowledge the costs of legal laxity: Restrictions on intelligence gathering may well have impeded the investigation of Zacarias Moussaoui, the "twentieth hijacker," before 9/11. David Cole, one of the movement's favorite law professors, goes so far as to lament that U.S. law makes "mere membership in a terrorist group grounds for exclusion and deportation."

And while civil libertarians may scant the value of Patriot, terrorists do not. Jeffrey Battle, an accused member of a terrorist cell in Portland, complained about Patriot in a recorded phone call that was recently released in court. People were less willing to provide financial support, he said, now that they were more likely to be punished for it.

Speaking of the administration's civil-liberties record, Al Gore said . . . that President Bush has "taken the most fateful step in the direction of [a] Big Brother nightmare that any president has ever allowed to occur." Dick Armey worries about "the lust for power that these people in the Department of Justice have." The civil-liberties debate could use a lot less rhetoric of this sort—and a lot more attention to detail.

A calm look at the Patriot Act shows that it's less of a threat to civil liberties than, say, campaign-finance reform. A lot of the controversy is the result of confusion. Opponents of the Patriot Act are fond of complaining that few people have bothered to read it. No kidding.

"[Patriot Act] provisions . . . gave FBI agents the authority to engage in fishing expeditions to see what Americans read."

The Patriot Act Threatens Library Patron Privacy

Bernie Sanders

In the following viewpoint U.S. representative Bernie Sanders, the longest-serving independent in the history of the House of Representatives, claims that the Patriot Act threatens the right of Americans to use libraries without fear that the government is monitoring their reading habits. The act grants the FBI the authority to obtain library records without showing any evidence that a library patron is involved in terrorist activities, he argues. Moreover, Sanders maintains, librarians asked to turn over records are not allowed to tell patrons a search was conducted. Since the FBI has abused its authority in the past, he contends, its power must be checked, not expanded.

As you read, consider the following questions:

1. In what two ways did the Patriot Act expand FBI authority, in Sanders's view?
2. What evidence, in Sanders's opinion, proves that the FBI has already used its new powers?
3. According to the author, what will the Freedom to Read Protection Act establish?

Bernie Sanders, "Unpatriotic Act," *Publishers Weekly*, vol. 250, August 18, 2003, p. 22. Copyright © 2003 by Reed Publishing USA. Reproduced from *Publishers Weekly*, published by the Bowker Magazine Group of Cahners Publishing Co., a division of Reed Publishing USA, by permission.

An unnecessary chill has descended on the nation's libraries and bookstores: the books you buy and read are now subject to government inspection and review.

After [the terrorist attack of September 11, 2001], the Bush administration, particularly Atty. Gen. John Ashcroft, pushed hard for passage of the USA Patriot Act, which contained sweeping changes to our nation's surveillance laws and new intelligence powers for the FBI and other agencies. At that time of national outrage, Congress passed with little debate a bill the attorney general had crafted.

Few who voted for the Patriot Act—I did not—knew that among its provisions was one that gave FBI agents the authority to engage in fishing expeditions to see what Americans read. Although it does not mention bookstores or libraries specifically, the sweeping legislation gives the FBI the power to seize all of the circulation, purchasing and other records of library users and bookstore customers on no stronger a claim than an FBI official's statement that they are part of a terrorism investigation. Surely the powers the government needs to fight terrorism can be subject to more meaningful checks and balances than that, especially when the right to read without government intrusion is at stake.

Expanding FBI Authority

Until the Patriot Act, the FBI had the authority to obtain bank records, credit records and certain other commercial records only upon some showing that the records requested related to a suspected member of a terrorist group. The Patriot Act expanded the FBI's authority in two ways. First, it gave the FBI the authority to seize any records of any entity—including libraries and bookstores. Second, Congress dropped the requirement that the FBI actually have some evidence that the person whose records it sought was a member of a terrorist group or otherwise involved in terrorism.

Now, one Patriot Act provision allows the FBI to obtain whole databases, including records of citizens not suspected of any wrongdoing. The FBI has a history of abusing its power: monitoring, keeping records on and infiltrating civil rights organizations, protest groups and others that had broken no laws but were considered controversial. Little has changed to prevent the FBI from abusing its powers again if it is left unchecked. The new powers appear to have been used already—a University of Illinois survey shows libraries were targeted at least 175 times in the year after 9/11—yet the FBI refuses to explain how or why.

Reading over Patrons' Shoulders

Ever since the U.S.A. PATRIOT Act was passed by Congress in October 2001, the FBI has been reading over our shoulders by visiting libraries across the country to demand library patrons' reading records and other files. Under the PATRIOT Act, the FBI doesn't have to demonstrate "probable cause" of criminal activity to request records; in fact, the so-called search warrant is issued by a secret court. Once granted, it entitles the FBI to procure any library records pertaining to book circulation, Internet use, or patron registration. Librarians can even be compelled to cooperate with the FBI in monitoring Internet usage.

Zara Gelsey, *Humanist*, September/October 2002.

Such is the state of affairs that librarians across the country are putting up signs warning patrons that the FBI may be snooping among their records. These librarians, along with booksellers, are particularly concerned because the proceeding for these warrants takes place in a closed court and the new law has a built-in gag order: those who are asked to turn over records are not allowed to say that the search has occurred or that records were given to the government. In addition, judges are not allowed to determine whether there is probable cause to justify such sweeping searches.

We need law enforcement to track down terrorists. But if we give up some of our most cherished freedoms—the right to read what we want without surveillance; the need for "probable cause" before searches are made—the terrorist attacks will have struck at the very heart of our constitutional rights.

To remedy the excesses of the Patriot Act that threaten our right to read, I have introduced the Freedom to Read Protection Act.[1] The bill, which has the support of Demo-

---

1. As of this writing the bill remains in the House Judiciary Committee.

crats and Republicans, progressives and conservatives, will establish once again that libraries and bookstores are no place for fishing expeditions. This new legislation will allow the FBI to use the constitutional routes at its disposal, including criminal subpoenas, to get library and bookstore records. At the same time, it will require—as had always been the case—that investigations be focused and that the reasons behind them be subject to judicial scrutiny. Booksellers, publishers and all other interested parties should check my Web site (www.bernie.house.gov) for regular updates about the progress of this legislation.

Before Congress begins any discussion of new powers for the FBI, as some in Washington are advocating, we must first focus on correcting the unchecked authority the Patriot Act already grants the government.

*"FBI investigators have exercised . . .
authority to obtain records with the utmost
respect for privacy."*

The Patriot Act Protects Library Patron Privacy

Robert S. Mueller

Robert S. Mueller, director of the Federal Bureau of Investigation (FBI), argues in the following viewpoint that the Patriot Act does not grant the FBI the authority to violate library patron privacy. Mueller grants that the act allows the FBI to obtain library records in the course of a terrorism investigation, but he maintains that congressional committees and oversight boards monitor the FBI's activities to guard against abuses. According to Mueller, the FBI will protect privacy and civil liberties while fighting the war on terrorism.

As you read, consider the following questions:
1. According to Mueller, what are some of the checks that prevent abuse or overreaching by FBI agents?
2. What, in Mueller's opinion, proves that the FBI has not used its investigative tools to invade the privacy of library patrons?
3. What FBI investigation demonstrates that libraries occasionally attract individuals involved in criminal conduct, in the author's view?

Robert S. Mueller, "On My Mind: The FBI and America's Libraries," *American Libraries*, vol. 35, January 2004, pp. 48–49. Copyright © 2004 by the American Library Association. Reproduced by permission.

L ibraries occupy a special place in American society. They contribute significantly to the First Amendment goal of an open marketplace for ideas by serving as a gateway to knowledge for all Americans, regardless of race, creed, affluence, or educational level.

The American Library Association [ALA] and other organizations have expressed concern that the FBI may use the powers it obtained in the USA Patriot Act in ways that are antithetical to libraries' traditional role in this country. I assure you that nothing could be further from the truth, and I thank the ALA for giving me this opportunity to continue a dialogue that began with my meeting in February [2003] with Washington Office Executive Director Emily Sheketoff to correct that misperception.

Section 215 of the Patriot Act permits law enforcement agents to request a court order so that they may secretly obtain records of any kind—including library records—in the course of "an investigation to protect against international terrorism or clandestine intelligence activities." Some have suggested that providing FBI counterterrorism investigators with the power to obtain library records through secret court order simply invites the government to maintain files documenting the books that one borrows from a library. Let me assure everyone that FBI investigators have exercised—and will continue to exercise—our authority to obtain records with the utmost respect for privacy, civil liberties, and the important role libraries play in this nation.

A System of Checks

We operate within a system that has a variety of checks to prevent abuse or overreaching. Agents can only seek a Section 215 order if the records being sought relate to an authorized counterintelligence or counterterrorism investigation. In regard to U.S. persons (citizens or permanent resident aliens), such investigations cannot be predicated solely on the exercise of First Amendment activities related to libraries. Guidelines promulgated by the Attorney General unequivocally provide that no investigation may be pursued regarding a U.S. person based solely on activities protected by the First Amendment or the lawful exercise of other rights secured by the Constitution or U.S. law.

Our compliance with the Attorney General's guidelines is monitored by numerous entities, including the Senate and House Intelligence Committees, the Intelligence Oversight Board of the President's Foreign Intelligence Advisory Board, the FBI's Inspection Division, the FBI's Office of Professional Responsibility, and the Department of Justice's Inspector General. This rigorous regime of self-regulation and third-party over-sight rightfully leaves no latitude for "fishing expeditions" in libraries, bookstores, or elsewhere.

Finding Evidence in Library Records

History shows libraries are included [in the Patriot Act] for good reason. In the 1997 Gianni Versace murder case, the 1990 Zodiac gunman investigation, and the hunt for the Unabomber, law enforcement officials sought records from specific libraries, which produced important evidence in those cases. Since the Patriot Act merely authorizes the court to issue similar orders in national security investigations, an amendment to exempt libraries completely from the Act would make such facilities a safe haven for terrorists.

Edwin Meese, *Washington Times*, July 8, 2004.

Moreover, from the day training begins for new FBI agents, they are steeped in the principles underlying the First and Fourth Amendments to the U.S. Constitution, the rules of criminal procedure, and the concepts underlying the Privacy Act. That training informs the investigative decisions that FBI agents and supervisors make every day and ensures that we responsibly employ the investigative tools that Congress has granted to the FBI.

Our experience with Section 215 orders demonstrates that we have not used our investigative tools to invade the privacy of library patrons. The FBI to date has not sought a single order pursuant to Section 215 directed at libraries. Moreover, in response to concerns that were raised last year [2003] by ALA and others about the possible targeting of libraries in terrorism investigations, we conducted an informal survey of our field offices. The results indicated that, following 9/11, the majority of FBI contacts with libraries were either to check out specific terrorism leads or to respond to reports of suspicious behavior by patrons.

Criminals in Libraries

We must recognize, however, that libraries and their services occasionally attract individuals involved in criminal conduct, including terrorism and espionage. For example, one piece of circumstantial evidence against Theodore Kaczynski, the so-called Unabomber, was obtained from a library. The Unabomber, who was at the time unidentified, sent a manuscript to the *New York Times* with an offer to cease terrorist actions if the paper would print the manuscript. Included within the manuscript were references to an obscure book, *The Ancient Engineers*, by L. Sprague De Camp. A librarian in Montana near Kaczynski's home told FBI agents that Kaczynski had ordered "tons of stuff" on L. Sprague De Camp. Kaczynski was subsequently arrested and convicted for his role in a string of bombings.

Another example arose in 2001 when Brian Regan, an employee of the National Reconnaissance Office, used computers at public libraries in northern Virginia and Maryland to research the purchase of false identification and to set up visits to foreign embassies. Regan was subsequently arrested and convicted of attempting to sell national security secrets to officials in those foreign embassies. Just as we investigate criminal conduct occurring in a home or at an Internet cafe, we must also investigate such conduct when it occurs in a public library.

I am personally committed to fighting the war on terrorism without violating the principles of civil liberty and privacy that make this country great. I sincerely hope that my comments here will give the ALA membership a better appreciation for the respect we have for libraries and for the right of patrons to enjoy libraries without fear of undue intrusion by the government.

I want to thank American Libraries for giving me this opportunity to address your concerns, and I look forward to continued discussion about this and any other issues with the ALA leadership in the future.

"[The Patriot Act] permits enforcement officials to obtain such information as web addresses, e-mail addresses, and session times based on a lower standard."

The Patriot Act Threatens Internet Privacy

Steven A. Osher

The Patriot Act threatens the privacy of American Internet users, argues Steven A. Osher in the following viewpoint. The act grants the federal government broad police power to issue warrants to obtain Internet records without proof that the person targeted is involved in a terrorist plot, he claims. Moreover, Osher maintains that while people may not expect their Internet addresses to be private, they rightly expect the content of their e-mail to be. Osher is a medical malpractice attorney in Miami, Florida.

As you read, consider the following questions:

1. According to Osher, why does a great deal of the Patriot Act focus on the Internet?
2. In the author's view, how does the FBI respond to concerns that both the content and the address are received when e-mail messages are intercepted?
3. What is one of the most far-reaching effects of the Patriot Act, in the author's opinion?

Steven A. Osher, "Privacy, Computers and the Patriot Act: The Fourth Amendment Isn't Dead, but No One Will Insure It," *Florida Law Review*, vol. 54, July 2002, pp. 521–42.

The tragic events of September 11, 2001 shocked the nation with their incomprehensible devastation and the stunning message of America's domestic vulnerability. At no time in recent memory, if ever, had Americans felt so threatened on their own soil. Because this was not the act of any identifiable geographic state, America was initially powerless to retaliate using its unparalleled military forces. Clearly, however, urgent measures were needed to restore domestic security. Congress quickly responded with the Uniting and Strengthening America by Providing Appropriate Tools Required to Intercept and Obstruct Terrorism Act, commonly known as the USA PATRIOT Act (USAPA)

This Essay examines the USAPA, in particular its effects on cyber communications and Fourth Amendment guarantees against unreasonable searches and seizures. . . .

The chief areas examined in this Essay concern the expansion of surveillance powers in wiretaps, search warrants, and subpoenas. Many of these have not only been expanded, but threshold requirements have been either lowered or removed for many types of searches by broadening the scope of the Foreign Intelligence Surveillance Act (FISA). Additionally, judicial approval for many searches has been reduced to a rubber stamp if the request is properly submitted.

The Dangers of Cyber Crime

A great deal of the USAPA focuses on the Internet. This may be due to the extreme danger cyber crimes pose to the economy and to the Department of Defense (DOD), which maintains a network of over two million computers, 10,000 local area networks, and 100 long-distance networks, which handle 95% of military communications. In 1999 alone the DOD was the target of 22,126 detected attacks, which may have represented only a small percentage of actual intrusions. Nearly all of the attempted unauthorized entries were the work of "fledgling hackers" who target the DOD because of the prestige of evading its protections. But whether hackers or terrorists, the danger is real. . . .

The dangers of cyber crime are difficult to overstate. Though not agents of any hostile power, many amateur hackers will publish the classified information that they are able to access in order to demonstrate their hacking abilities. This permits the information to be accessed by anyone, including potential enemies. Also, terrorists could disrupt military operations by substituting munitions orders for other supplies such as light bulbs, thereby tendering military installations unprepared for combat.

According to the FBI, in addition to the threat to national defense, electronic crime costs more than ten billion dollars per year. Many businesses that are targeted never realize that they have been victimized, and of those, many simply do not report the crimes for fear of negative publicity. The perpetrators of electronic crimes are elusive and may operate from anywhere in the world.

On October 26, 2001, at the signing of the USAPA, President [George W.] Bush addressed the novel issues raised by new technology and the government's response:

> As of today, we're changing the laws governing information-sharing. And as importantly, we're changing the culture of our various agencies that fight terrorism. Countering and investigating terrorist activity is the number one priority for both law enforcement and intelligence agencies.

> Surveillance of communications is another essential tool to pursue and stop terrorists. The existing law was written in the era of rotary telephones. This new law that I sign today will allow surveillance of all communications used by terrorists, including e-mails, the Internet, and cell phones.

> As of today, we'll be able to better meet the technological challenges posed by this proliferation of communications technology. Investigations are often slowed by limits on the reach of federal search warrants. Law enforcement agencies have to get a new warrant for each new district they investigate, even when they're after the same suspect.

> Under this new law, warrants are valid across all districts and across all states.

Challenges to Fourth Amendment Protection

The Fourth Amendment requires that a search warrant specify the "place to be searched." In order to search a place other than that specified, a new search warrant typically must be obtained. While the primary effect of this "particularity" requirement is to eliminate general warrants, it also prevents law enforcement authorities from "forum shop-ping" by only giving the judge in the relevant jurisdiction the discretion to grant or deny the request for a warrant. But, section 216 of the USAPA permits a judge or magistrate to issue a pen register or trap and trace order that does not specify the Internet service provider (ISP), leaving it to the law enforcement officer to insert one or more ISPs of his choice. This order is valid anywhere in the United States. An ancillary effect of this provision is that if an ISP challenges the effect of the order, it must present the challenge in the jurisdiction where the order was issued, which could be across the country. With little to gain, few ISPs are likely to bring such a challenge.

In *Smith v. Maryland* the Supreme Court ruled that the installation and use of a pen register was not a search under the Fourth Amendment. A pen register is defined as "a me-chanical device that records the numbers dialed on a tele-phone by monitoring the electrical impulses caused when the dial on the telephone is released." In *Smith* the defen-dant appealed his robbery conviction that was based on in-criminating telephone company records. Following the rob-bery, the defendant had made repeated telephone calls to his victim. Based on information obtained from the telephone company pen register, police obtained a search warrant for his residence that yielded incriminating evidence.

On appeal, the defendant sought to exclude "all fruits de-rived from the pen register" because the police installed the device without a warrant. The Court, in a 5-4 decision, held that there was "no constitutionally protected reasonable ex-pectation of privacy in the numbers dialed into a telephone system and hence no search within the Fourth Amendment."

Applying the Law to the Internet

Before the passage of the USAPA, there was considerable debate about the applicability of the *Smith* pen register cat-egorization to the Internet. Section 216 of the USAPA sim-ply inserts the appropriate language to analogize the routing of electronic communications on the Internet to the dialing of a phone. This permits enforcement officials to obtain such information as web addresses, e-mail addresses, and session times based on a lower standard than the probable cause necessary for a search warrant; the agent must merely certify that the information is "relevant to an ongoing criminal investigation." The USAPA obligates the court to issue the warrant if this basic requirement is met.

But the analogy to telephone records is flawed. In order to appreciate the distinction, a basic understanding of the Internet is helpful. Rather than directly linking all of the computers of users, the Internet is able to function as it does by employing a technology known as packet switching. This technology breaks data down into small packets of information, which are then transmitted and reassembled in the correct order at the destination computer. The packets are encoded at the source for correct reassembly, permitting them to utilize the most efficient routing along the way.

Casting a Wide Net

The Patriot Act is complex and powerful. It broadens the definition of terrorism and increases the penalties for terrorism.

Some of the more sweeping changes involve electronic surveillance. The act permits federal investigators to use more-powerful tools to monitor phone calls, e-mail messages, and even Web surfing. We all hope that means agents will be better able to arrest terrorists and foil their plans. But the changes also mean we now have even less guarantee of privacy on the Net. The new law, along with new surveillance tools, will create a dragnet wide enough that anyone's e-mail note, text chat, or search inquiry might be snared.

Anne Kandra, *PC World*, January 2002.

The *Smith* opinion, citing *United States v. New York Telephone Co.*, reasoned that pen register-supplied information was not private because "[i]t does not overhear oral communications and does not indicate whether calls are actually completed." Conversely, because the information contained in e-mail messages is transmitted in packets, whoever intercepts the message must separate the address from the contents of the e-mail. The FBI responds to invasion of privacy concerns by asserting that they can be trusted to separate address from content and retain only the former.

Perhaps the *Smith* decision would have been different if telephone numbers were spoken into the receiver, rather than dialed, and law enforcement officials had to separate the numbers from the remainder of the conversation. Even without these issues, the *Smith* dissent was bitter in its concern for Fourth Amendment guarantees. Justices Stewart and Brennan worried that "[t]he information captured by such surveillance emanates from private conduct within a person's home or office—locations that without question are entitled to Fourth and Fourteenth Amendment protection." The *Smith* case has been frequently criticized for its narrowing of the expectation of privacy. . . .

A Threat to Privacy

With the enactment of the USAPA, the government has enacted such provisions, many of which are being criticized as "alien to well-recognized Fourth Amendment freedoms." Considering that today many people maintain their "papers and effects" on their computer hard drives, the expansion of pen register authority to include electronic communications and Internet usage can "mean the collection of information more private than IP addresses, which are roughly the Net's equivalent of phone numbers."

Attorney General John Ashcroft argues that roving wiretaps, which are permitted by section 206 of the USAPA, do not violate the Fourth Amendment because they "do not eliminate the particularity requirement[s] for search warrants; [they] merely substitute particularity of person for particularity of place." The Government contends that it will concentrate its surveillance only on the target of the investigation, but in reality all conversations, including those conducted by third parties, will be wiretapped. To use one example, "if the government suspects that a particular target uses different pay phones at Boston's Logan Airport, then the government would have the power to wire all the public telephones at Logan Airport and the discretion to decide which conversations to monitor."

In *Steagald v. United States*, police

> relied on the warrant (arrest warrant for Ricky Lyons) as legal authority to enter the home of a third person based on

their belief that Ricky Lyons might be a guest there. . . . [W]hile the warrant in this case may have protected Lyons from an unreasonable seizure, it did absolutely nothing to protect petitioner's privacy interest in being free from an unreasonable invasion and search of his home.

Not only do roving telephone wiretaps invade the expectation of privacy of uncounted third parties, but the extension of roving surveillance to the computer equipment of a target also subjects "the e-mail messages of thousands of individuals [writes Tracey Maclin]" to government search. Because government agents can now decide when, where, and how often to monitor communications, *Steagald* strongly suggests that this expansion of the government's power to monitor its citizens runs counter to the Fourth Amendment, which "was intended to check, and not expand, police power and discretion.". . .

Questioning the Patriot Act

Among the myriad troubling questions associated with the USAPA, the most fundamental is whether there was a need for it at all. The government never argued that the legal restraints on law enforcement authorities prevented them from stopping the terrorists of September 11th, or from investigating the crime. The FBI already had the power and the technology to monitor telephone and Internet communications in situations involving air piracy and the destruction of aircraft, as well as under the FISA. Existing law provided for roving wiretaps if law enforcement agents could demonstrate that the target of the investigation was changing phones in order to thwart detection. The government could already wiretap any person suspected of working for a foreign government or organization. The government already had "sneak and peek" authority to search without notification, if certain criteria were met: if an agent demonstrated that either an individual's safety would be endangered, someone would flee, evidence would be destroyed, witnesses would be intimidated or an investigation would otherwise be jeopardized or delayed, this authority could be granted.

One of the most far-reaching effects of the USAPA is the

removal of the review of a "neutral and detached magistrate" from the process of citizen surveillance. Many of the provisions that do involve some judicial oversight require that the order be granted if the application is properly filled out. Under the broader FISA provisions that now apply to the investigation of domestic crimes under the USAPA, no probable cause is necessary to justify an intelligence wiretap.

Many of the provisions of the USAPA are disturbingly vague. Section 808 expands the definition of terrorism to crimes "relating to protection of computers." This language could encompass a wide range of offenses unrelated to terrorism, such as the sale of software that fails to perform correctly, posting incorrect or misleading content on web pages, and deceptive Internet marketing schemes. While these all may be serious problems, they do not merit the abrogation of constitutional liberties.

Many critics question the motivation behind the USAPA. Senator Feingold said that the USAPA "goes into a lot of areas that have nothing to do with terrorism and have a lot to do with the government and the FBI having a wish list of things they want to do." A principal concern of critics is the broad expansion of FISA surveillance authority, allowing its use in primarily criminal investigations. This has the effect of converting the FBI's mission from solving crime to intelligence gathering and effectively "put[s] the CIA back in the business of spying on Americans." The USAPA also creates the new crime of "domestic terrorism" that could transform protesters into terrorists if they are associated with conduct that endangers human life.

No Increase in Security

Others are skeptical about the promised benefit of increased security. Carole Samdup, spokesperson for Democracy and Rights, claims "[a]ll this technology has existed for years and we still haven't arrested anyone (using it). . . . Even Timothy McVeigh was under surveillance." Boaz Guttman, former terrorism investigator in the Israeli police force, downplays the utility of technologies such as Carnivore, a program that monitors and filters all electronic communications in search of particular terms.

There is no miracle at all with wiretapping. It did not prevent crime even in Red Russia. What if terrorists use coded messages. He [sic] calls the bomb "cake" and the target "my mother in law." You can intercept 'til tomorrow, 'til next week [and not stop terrorism]. . . . If somebody thinks that with all this tracing alone, he will defeat terror, as I said to an important person in your country, "Sorry, you are sleeping in the middle of the day."

More fundamentally, the focus of the USAPA on expanding government surveillance is misguided, because the underlying assumption that the attacks of September 11 resulted from the government's limited power to collect information is erroneous. For example, after the 1993 bombing of the World Trade Center, the FBI discovered that it already had in its possession detailed plans and maps of the attack at the time it occurred. The history of intelligence indicates that most failures result from a lack of proper implementation of procedures already in place, rather than the need for new procedures.

A History of Abuse

No restraint was ever placed on government power without a history of government abuse. As far back as 1706 the Framers were aware of the dangers of multiple-specific search warrants, after colonial officials used them to search every home in New Hampshire. Congressional concern led to the Collection Act of 1789, which limited federal searches to single structures and eliminated "wide-ranging exploratory searches."

Because these limitations are intended to remedy government overreaching, no one ever proposes lifting governmental restraints until the memory of abuse has time to fade, usually a generation or two after the excesses. No doubt the future will bring vivid reminders of the original reasons for the restraints that Congress has so hastily lifted from the powers of the government over its citizens.

Ironically, blanket monitoring of citizens could have the same chilling effect on democracy that terrorism does. Justice Marshall, dissenting in *Smith*, remarked that

[p]ermitting governmental access to telephone records on less than probable cause may . . . impede certain forms of politi-

cal affiliation and journalistic endeavor that are the hallmark of a truly free society. Particularly given the Government's previous reliance on warrantless telephonic surveillance to trace reporters' sources and monitor protected political activity, I am unwilling to insulate use of pen registers from independent judicial review.

One imagines what Justice Marshall would have said about the legislation before us.

Daniel Bryant, Assistant Attorney General for the Department of Justice, observed that "[a]s the Commander-In-Chief, the President must be able to use whatever means necessary to prevent attacks upon the United States; this power, by implication, includes the authority to collect information necessary for its effective exercise." No one can gainsay this; however, the means utilized by the President must be subject to constitutional constraints. The President is not above the law and not above the Constitution.

Civil liberties are anathema to government. Since the first collectivization of humans, governments have jealously guarded their powers, only reluctantly ceding increments of control to their subjects. That is the miracle of America. In spite of historical excesses, this nation has always returned to the principles of human rights and guarantees envisioned by the Founding Fathers.

Justice Brennan, in his 1987 address to the Law School of Hebrew University in Jerusalem, expressed frustration at America's episodic abandonment of civil liberties in times of crisis. Justice Brennan noted that "[a]fter each perceived security crisis ended, the United States has remorsefully realized that the abrogation of civil liberties was unnecessary. But it has proven unable to prevent itself from repeating the error when the next crisis came along."

There is no doubt that the expanded powers incorporated into the USAPA will be used improperly, especially given the limited oversight provisions. Political enemies will be targets of espionage; embarrassing information about select individuals will once again be "leaked." Perhaps terrorists will even be freed after incriminating evidence is suppressed on constitutional grounds (if they manage to obtain a civil trial).

Eventually, the stories of governmental excess will be

publicized, and the public will realize the damage that has been done to personal privacy. This has already occurred with well-meaning legislation such as RICO and other asset forfeiture provisions that have succeeded in injuring average citizens while failing to remedy the problems they were intended to address. History shows that individuals will suffer gravely before the damage is recognized, and once again America will realize that a society that sacrifices its freedom for security achieves neither.

"[The pen register amendments to the Patriot Act] added to the privacy of Internet communications, rather than subtracted from it."

The Patriot Act Enhances Internet Privacy

Orin S. Kerr

According to Orin S. Kerr in the following viewpoint, the Patriot Act does not expand police power over Internet usage; it increases Internet privacy protection. Prior to the act law enforcement could tap the Internet without restriction because privacy law only provided protection in regards to phone taps. The Patriot Act broadens the law to include Internet taps, which now require a court order. Thus the act creates privacy protection for the Internet while also giving law enforcement a tool to trace terrorist activities. Kerr, a law professor at George Washington University Law School, worked in the Department of Justice Computer Crime and Intellectual Property Section.

As you read, consider the following questions:

1. In Kerr's opinion, what features make broad characterizations of the Patriot Act difficult to make?
2. According to the author, why was it difficult before the Patriot Act to determine whether the terms "pen register" and "trap and trace" device applied to the Internet?
3. What do critics of the pen register amendments of the Patriot Act ignore, in the author's view?

Orin S. Kerr, "Internet Surveillance Law After USA Patriot Act: The Big Brother That Isn't," *Northwestern University Law Review*, vol. 97, 2003. Copyright © 2003 by Northwestern University School of Law. Reproduced by permission.

The passage of the USA Patriot Act on October 26, 2001 has been widely portrayed as a dark moment for the civil liberties of Internet users. The ACLU [American Civil Liberties Union] declared that the Act gave law enforcement "extraordinary new powers." Another civil liberties group, the Electronic Frontier Foundation, announced that "the civil liberties of ordinary Americans have taken a tremendous blow with this law." The website of the Electronic Privacy Information Center featured a drawing of a tombstone that stated "The Fourth Amendment: 1789–2001." Major media outlets agreed. The *New York Times* viewed the Act as an overreaction to [the September 11, 2001, terrorist attacks], and concluded that the law gave the government unjustified "broad new powers." The *Washington Post* also opposed the Act: its editorial board described the Patriot Act as "panicky legislation" that "reduce[d] the healthy oversight of the courts." The unanimous verdict was that the Patriot Act created a sweeping and probably unjustifiable expansion of law enforcement authority in cyberspace.

Is this verdict justified? To answer this, it is crucial to recognize that the Patriot Act is not a single coherent law. The Act collected hundreds of minor amendments to federal law, grouped into ten subparts or "Titles," on topics ranging from immigration to money laundering. With many of these amendments, the devil is in the details: especially in the electronic surveillance context, the complex relationship among sections of statutory text means that the changes often defy easy soundbites. Further, the language that passed on October 26th differed in significant ways from the language the Justice Department first proposed just a few days after September 11th. The congressional negotiations that ensured the quick passage of the Patriot Act led to many compromises, and even considerable victories for the Act's opponents. Altogether, these features make broad characterizations of the Patriot Act difficult to maintain.

Focusing on Internet Surveillance

When we focus on the Internet surveillance provisions that passed into law, however, it becomes clear that the popular understanding of the Patriot Act is substantially wrong. The

Patriot Act did not tilt the balance between Internet privacy and security strongly in favor of security. Most of the Patriot Act's key changes reflected reasonable compromises that updated antiquated laws. Some of these changes advance law enforcement interests, but others advance privacy interests, and several do both at the same time. None challenged the basic legal framework that Congress created in 1986 to protect Internet privacy. Studying the Internet surveillance provisions of the Act suggests that the media portrayal of the Patriot Act as "extraordinary" and "panicky legislation" has little in common with the law Congress actually enacted. . . .

[This viewpoint] will explore one of the most controversial provisions of the Patriot Act: the amendments making the pen register[1] law applicable to the Internet. The pen register law has governed prospective envelope surveillance[2] of the telephone since Congress enacted [the Electronic Communications Privacy Act of] 1986, and the Patriot Act makes clear that this law also applies to the Internet. The press uniformly presented this change as a significant expansion of law enforcement authority. The *Washington Post* stated that this change "makes it easier for the government to engage in wiretapping by, in effect, lowering the standard of judicial review." The *New York Times* described this change as a grant of "broad authority to inspect logs of Internet use and the address fields of email messages." Both the political left and the political right agreed that this was a significant and potentially dangerous change. On the left, the *New Republic* thundered that this change gave the government "essentially unlimited authority to install recording devices" to monitor the Internet. On the right, a group of lawyers affiliated with the Federalist Society approved of the Patriot Act as a whole, but singled out the pen register amendments as the only troubling change to the electronic surveillance laws. . . .

These criticisms of the Patriot Act are unfounded. The pen

---

1. A pen register is a device that records the telephone numbers dialed from the telephone to which it is attached.   2. Envelope surveillance of the telephone includes recording the phone numbers calling in to a tapped phone and the numbers dialed out from a tapped phone, which is distinguished from surveillance of the content of the telephone call. Envelope is a term used to distinguish addresses and phone numbers from the contents of letters and telephone conversations.

register amendments to the Patriot Act do not signal an unwarranted expansion of law enforcement authority. To the contrary, the changes reaffirm existing law that aligns Internet surveillance law with postal and telephone surveillance. More importantly, to the extent that the amendments actually changed the law at all, on the whole they probably added to the privacy of Internet communications, rather than subtracted from it. Ironically, the pen register amendments that have been portrayed as unwarranted expansions of law enforcement authority are neither unwarranted, nor even expansions of authority. This does not mean that Congress could not increase the privacy protections of the pen register law in the future; it could, and I think it probably should. However, it turns out that the Patriot Act is not the source of the problem, but rather the first step toward a better solution. . . .

Envelope Surveillance Law

Although Congress has enacted statutory privacy protections that govern network surveillance, Congress historically has shown little interest in protecting mere envelope information. Congress has regulated prospective content information very strictly, with a warrant requirement in the case of the postal system, and a super-warrant requirement for telephones and the Internet. However, mere envelope information has traditionally received little if any protection in communications networks such as the postal system and the telephone. . . .

What about the Internet? More specifically, in the period leading up to the Patriot Act, what privacy laws regulated the prospective surveillance of envelope information in the case of email surveillance and packet surveillance?[3] The answer is surprisingly unclear. The only law that could conceivably have applied was the pen register statute, but it provided an odd mix of telephone-specific language and more

3. Packet surveillance divides Internet communication into envelope information and content information. When a computer sends information across the Internet, it breaks the communication into packets and creates a "packet header" to direct the packet to its destination. The packet header contains addressing information including the Internet Protocol (IP) address and the type of packet it is. When the packet arrives, the receiving computer discards the packet header and keeps the original message, the content, called the packet's "payload."

general text. The statute divided the category of envelope information into two subcategories: the "to" addressing information, which historically would be obtained by installing a pen register, and the "from" addressing information, which historically would be obtained by running a "trap and trace." Rather than refer to the information to be gathered, the structure of the pen register law prohibited the installation or use of a pen register or trap and trace device without a court order.

Before the Patriot Act, however, the definitions of the terms "pen register" and "trap and trace device" did not make clear whether they applied only to the telephone, or whether they could also apply to the Internet. The definition of "trap and trace device" was quite broad: it referred to "a device which captures the incoming electronic or other impulses which identify the originating number of an instrument or device from which a wire or electronic communication was transmitted." Given that most Internet communications are "electronic communication[s]," this definition appeared to apply to the Internet as well as to the phone system. In contrast, the definition of "pen register" appeared strikingly telephone-specific: the law defined a pen register as "a device which records or decodes electronic or other impulses which identify the numbers dialed or otherwise transmitted on the telephone line to which such device is attached."

Applying the Law to the Internet

So did the pen register laws apply to the Internet? The Justice Department believed they did and that the pen register laws regulated both Internet email and packet-level envelope surveillance just as they did telephone envelope surveillance. In fact, Justice Department practice had embraced the pen register statute for several years as the means of conducting Internet envelope surveillance. Federal judges had at least implicitly agreed: judges had signed pen register orders authorizing Internet email and packet surveillance hundreds, if not thousands, of times in the years leading up to the Patriot Act. While some magistrate judges had asked prosecutors whether the statute applied to the Internet, the judges always satisfied themselves that it did and signed the order. One magistrate judge in Los Angeles had also written an unpublished order agreeing that the statute applied to the Internet: "Although apparently not contemplated by the drafters of the original statute," Judge James McMahon wrote, "the use of a pen register order in the present situation is compatible with the terms of the statute." The text remained uncertain, but as a matter of law enforcement practice, it was generally understood that the pen register laws applied to the Internet.

Envelope and Content Information

Surveillance Type	Envelope Information	Content Information
Postal Mail	1) To, from mailing address of a letter	The contents of the letter
	2) Postmark, stamp	
	3) Color, size, weight of package	
Telephone	1) To, from telephone numbers for a call	The contents of the telephone [conversation]
Email	1) To, from email address for an email	The contents of the email, including the subject line
	2) Mail header info (length of email, digital postmarks) minus the subject line	
Internet Packets	1) To, from IP addresses	Payload of the packet (the contents of any communication between two computers)
	2) Remaining packet header information (length of packet, type of traffic)	

Orin S. Kerr, *Northwestern University Law Review*, 2003.

Notably, the government's conclusion that the pen register statute applied to the Internet created a double-edged sword. Without the pen register statute, the government could conduct envelope surveillance without a court order. The government or anybody else could wiretap the Internet and collect any noncontent information it wished without restriction. Applying the pen register laws to the Internet denied the government the power to conduct envelope surveillance without a court order, which limited government power and blocked private entities from conducting prospective envelope surveillance, thus protecting privacy. At the same time, applying the pen register statute to the Internet benefited law enforcement by giving the government a relatively easy way of obtaining orders compelling ISPs [Internet Service Providers] to conduct prospective envelope surveillance on the government's behalf. Absent that authority, the government would need to install monitoring devices itself, rely on the voluntary cooperation of ISPs, or try to use other laws requiring a higher factual showing than the pen register laws to obtain court orders compelling ISPs to conduct envelope surveillance. . . .

The Expansion of the Pen Register Laws

In the wake of the terrorist attacks on New York and Washington on September 11, 2001, pressure built on the Bush Administration to propose antiterrorism legislation. Just days after the attacks, Attorney General John Ashcroft contacted various divisions within DOJ [Department of Justice] and sought recommendations for legislative changes that could help fight the war on terrorism. One area that surfaced as a promising arena was Internet surveillance law. The DOJ had been clamoring for changes to the antiquated surveillance laws for years, and the September 11th attacks provided an obvious opportunity to update the laws. The link between the surveillance laws and terrorism was not direct because the September 11th attacks did not directly implicate the Internet. However, terrorists groups such as Al-Qaeda were known to favor the latest Internet technologies to communicate with each other, which meant that updating the Internet surveillance laws could assist law enforcement in terrorism-related cases. In any event, the obviously antiquated surveillance laws provided one of the few areas in which new laws were both clearly needed and could conceivably help the Justice Department fight terrorism. Further, the events of September 11th changed the political climate considerably, softening the opposition that had successfully blocked DOJ efforts to amend the Internet surveillance statutes in the previous Congress. . . .

Updating the pen register statute so that it clearly applied to the Internet provided one obvious priority. . . . The Justice Department's proposal aimed to do this in a minimalist way. Rather than rewrite the entire statute, the DOJ proposed to amend the definition of "pen register" and "trap and trace device" to make clear that it applied broadly to network envelope information, encompassing both telephones and the Internet. The DOJ proposed to describe envelope information as "dialing, routing, addressing, or signaling information" and to amend the definitions of pen register and trap and trace device to incorporate this broader definition. Congress essentially adopted the DOJ's approach in the Patriot Act, with the slight modification that the phrase "dialing, routing, addressing, or signaling information" was supplemented with a clarification that "such information shall not include the contents of any communication." This clarification to the DOJ's proposal was added at Senator [Patrick] Leahy's recommendation to ensure that the expanded pen register amendment did not trump the Wiretap Act [Electronic Communications Privacy Act of 1986].

Questioning the Criticism

As demonstrated earlier, the Patriot Act's modification of the pen register statute to include all "dialing, routing, addressing, or signaling information" proved to be one of the most controversial provisions in the Act. The media widely interpreted this change as a sweeping and unjustified expansion of law enforcement authority. To be fair, some of these reactions derived from the initial DOJ proposal, which lacked Senator Leahy's clarification that the changes to the scope of the pen register statute did not alter the scope of the Wiretap Act. . . . But even so, the criticisms of the pen register amendment prove surprisingly weak.

First, the criticisms ignore the fact that the pen register statute is primarily a privacy law. The law protects envelope information, making it a federal crime to collect envelope information without a court order. If the pen register statute did not apply to the Internet, then email and packet envelope surveillance would be totally unregulated by federal privacy law. In such a world, the government would be allowed to conduct envelope surveillance of the entire country's emails and Internet communications without a court order, or without even any prior authorization within the Executive Branch. Even more broadly, any private party would be allowed to do the same.

The Patriot Act's pen register amendments helped avert this situation by clarifying that the government was required to obtain a court order to conduct prospective envelope surveillance of Internet communications. In other words, the Patriot Act requires a court order, where before it may not have been necessary. From a civil libertarian standpoint, this is plainly a step in the right direction. Ironically, the real problem with the Patriot Act from a civil libertarian perspective is not that it goes too far, but that it does not go far enough in protecting the privacy of envelope information. Making it a crime to conduct envelope surveillance on the Internet without a court order is an improvement, but should have been matched with a higher threshold to obtain the court order that was required, combined with judicial review of the government's application. I would personally support such a change; I believe that a higher "specific and articulable facts" threshold would not add substantial burden for law enforcement, and at least on paper it would add privacy protection. However, the fact that this section of the Patriot Act could have offered stronger protection should not obscure the fact that as a whole the amendment helps add privacy protections, not reduce them.

Preexisting Practice

The criticisms of the pen register amendments also missed the mark because they failed to recognize that the changes codified a decade's worth of preexisting practice that had matched Internet privacy protections to telephone privacy protections. The Justice Department had been obtaining pen register orders to conduct envelope surveillance for years, and the new text explicitly recognized and approved the practice. The legislative change did not expand any authority. . . . Although styled a "change" in the law by its critics, the pen register amendments merely reaffirm the status quo. In itself this provides no reason to celebrate the amendments, as the status quo may be inadequate. However, the fact that the change reaffirms long-standing practice seems to undercut claims that the change dramatically expanded law enforcement powers.

Further, applying the pen register laws to the Internet matched the regulation of the Internet to the regulation of the telephone network and exceeded the protection that the law provides to similar surveillance of the postal network. After the Patriot Act, envelope surveillance of the telephone and the Internet requires a pen register order, whereas envelope surveillance of postal mail still requires no court order whatsoever. Although some believe that the standards for Internet envelope surveillance should be more strict than their analogues in the telephone context, at the very least the Patriot Act imposes same standard for analogous information in the case of the telephone, and more privacy protection for analogous information in the case of the postal network.

Criticisms of the pen register amendments also failed to note that the negotiations over the various bills that led to the Patriot Act actually added privacy protections to the pen register statute that prohibit the disclosure of information obtained through envelope surveillance. Prior to the Patriot Act, government officials could publish or leak information obtained by use of a pen register or trap and trace device. During the congressional negotiations, pro-privacy legislators managed to insert language that limits the disclosure of information obtained through prospective envelope surveillance of Internet and telephone communications to disclosures made "in the proper performance of the official functions of the officer or governmental entity making the disclosure." Any other disclosure is prohibited. Although the exact contours of this prohibition remain unclear, the new provision bolsters the privacy protections that the pen register statutes offer to envelope information.

Periodical Bibliography

The following articles have been selected to supplement the diverse views presented in this chapter.

Bob Barr	"Patriot Act Games: It Can Happen Here," *American Spectator*, August/September 2003.
Chip Berlet and Pam Chamberlain	"Resisting Repression: Executive Orders and Legislation Curtail Civil Liberties," *Resist*, July 2003.
Joseph Bottum	"The Library Lie," *Weekly Standard*, January 26, 2004.
Walt Brasch	"Freedom to Read Versus USA Patriot Act," *Liberal Opinion*, March 18, 2002.
Barbara Dority	"Your Every Move," *Humanist*, January/February 2004.
Electronic Frontier Foundation	"EFF Analysis of the Provisions of the USA PATRIOT Act That Relate to Online Activities," October 27, 2003, www.eff.org.
Zara Gelsey	"Who's Reading Over Your Shoulder?" *Humanist*, September/October 2002.
Kenneth Jost	"Civil Liberties Debates," *CQ Researcher*, October 24, 2003.
Frank Kramer	"Why the Patriot Act Worries Booksellers," *Boston Globe*, October 8, 2003.
Nancy Kranich	"The Impact of the USA PATRIOT Act on Free Expression," *Free Expression Policy Project*, May 5, 2003, www.fepproject.org.
Paul D. Lawrence	"Shredding the Bill of Rights," *People's Weekly World*, January/February 2004.
Pepi Leistyna	"You Have the Right to Remain Silent," *Resist*, July 2003.
Charles Levendosky	"Spying on What People Read Kills Their Curiosity," *Progressive Populist*, May 1, 2003.
Kate O'Beirne	"Congress's Patriotic Act: This Is a Law That Defends America and, Yes, Preserves Civil Liberties, Dammit," *National Review*, September 15, 2003.
Marcia S. Smith et al.	"The Internet and the USA PATRIOT Act: Potential Implications for Electronic Privacy, Security, Commerce, and Government," *Congressional Research Service*, March 4, 2002.

CHAPTER 3

Should the Patriot Act Be Amended?

Chapter Preface

As more Americans have begun to express their fear that the Patriot Act poses a threat to their civil liberties, congressional opponents of the act have responded by proposing legislation to limit its impact. These legislative proposals, submitted by conservative Republicans, liberal Democrats, and long-standing Independents alike, have met with opposition from other members of Congress and criticism from Patriot Act supporters.

One of the first legislative proposals to limit the scope of the Patriot Act came from Independent congressman Bernie Sanders of Vermont. In February 2003 Sanders decided to counter what he believes to be one of the most egregious provisions of the Patriot Act—Section 215. This section authorizes secret searches of a suspect's personal records without the target's knowledge. Sanders is particularly concerned about searches of library and bookstore records, claiming that such searches stifle the freedom to read. By the time he submitted the Freedom to Read Protection Act, Sanders had garnered 152 sponsors in the House, including both Democrats and Republicans. The act would exempt libraries and bookstores from Section 215 of the Patriot Act and would require a higher standard of proof than mere suspicion of criminal or terrorist activity for search warrants presented at libraries and bookstores. Legislation such as Sanders's Freedom to Read Protection Act has, however, often met with strong opposition by congressional leaders who support the Patriot Act. House leaders have rejected Sanders's requests to hold hearings on the bill, and an attempt to add the bill as an amendment to other legislation failed.

The most successful attempt to limit the impact of the Patriot Act as of this writing was made by conservative Republican congressman Butch Otter of Idaho. Otter successfully convinced the House in July 2003 to approve a prohibition on the use of federal funds for Section 213 "sneak and peek" searches. Section 213 search warrants are executed without the target's knowledge, and notice of the search is delayed. For example, Section 213 permits federal agents to search a suspect's home, plant a listening device, or copy a computer hard drive without notifying him or her until a later date. Otter's measure would prevent the spending of federal money to implement such covert, delayed-notification warrants. Although the proposal passed the House, in November 2003 Senate and House leaders refused to place that provision in the November 2003 spending bill, thus killing the proposal.

Some analysts contend that these attempts to limit the Patriot Act threaten law enforcement efforts to prosecute terrorists and prevent terrorist plots. James Jay Carafano and Paul Rosenzweig of the Heritage Foundation, a conservative think tank, maintain, "Instead of second-guessing the Patriot Act, Congress should focus on passing legislation to reauthorize the powers granted in the law that are due to sunset in 2005." These analysts contend that national security should be a priority. "Safeguarding the civil liberties of American citizens is vitally important, as important during war as during periods of peace," Carafano and Rosenzweig grant, "but so too is preserving our security. . . . Hysterical criticism that the Act was unnecessary and is a threat to a healthy civil society have proven unfounded, and calls for repeal or significant revisions are just wrongheaded."

Despite this criticism, Patriot Act opponents in Congress continue to propose legislation that limits the act. "What we are going to have to do is, brick by brick, take the most egregious parts out of the Patriot Act," Otter contends. Whether Congress will pass legislation amending the Patriot Act remains to be seen. In the following chapter authors express their views on the necessity of amending the act.

*"I'm starting . . . to call on the United
States Congress to renew the Patriot Act
and to make all of its provisions
permanent."*

The Patriot Act Should Be Expanded

George W. Bush

The Patriot Act gives law enforcement the tools it needs to fight terrorism and make America safe, claims President George W. Bush in the following viewpoint. Prior to the act, Bush asserts, fighting terrorism was more difficult because law enforcement agencies could not share information. The information-sharing provisions of the act have led to cooperation among these agencies, which in turn has helped them disrupt terrorist cells, he maintains. Therefore, Bush argues, Congress should not only make the act permanent, it should expand the act to include more tools to help law enforcement fight America's war on terrorism (the expanded act has sometimes been referred to as Patriot II). This viewpoint was originally given as a speech at the Hershey Lodge and Convention Center in Pennsylvania on April 19, 2004.

As you read, consider the following questions:
1. According to Bush, what tools used to investigate organized crime did the Patriot Act extend to terrorists?
2. In the author's opinion, why did Congress set some key provisions of the Patriot Act to expire?
3. Why is it difficult to protect America, in the author's view?

George W. Bush, address at Hershey Lodge and Convention Center, Hershey, Pennsylvania, April 19, 2004.

As we gather this afternoon we're 140 miles away from Shanksville, Pennsylvania. This is a place where many innocent lives ended [during the September 11, 2001, terrorist attacks]. Shanksville is also the place where American citizens stood up to evil, charged their attackers and began the first counter-offensive in the war on terror. Those passengers on Flight 93[1] showed that the spirit of America is strong and brave in the face of danger. And this nation will always honor their memory.

The best way to secure our homeland, the best way for us to do our duty, is to stay on the offensive against the terrorist network. We began the offense shortly after September the 11th. We're carrying out a broad strategy, a worldwide strategy to bring the killers to justice. The best way to secure America is to bring them to justice before they hurt us again, which is precisely what the United States of America will continue to do.

Two-thirds of known al Qaeda[2] leaders have been captured or killed. We're making progress. It's a different kind of war than the war that Major Dick Winters fought in.[3] This is a war against people who will hide in a cave; a war against people who hide in the shadows of remote cities, or big cities, and then they strike and they kill. And they kill innocent people. They have no—as I said, they have no conscience, they have no sense of guilt. But they also know we're on their trail. And they will find out there is no cave or hole deep enough to hide from American justice.

The Lessons of September 11

We must be determined in this, and we've got a lot of really good people, a lot of good people on the move. We're also working with nations from around the world, sharing intelligence, making it clear that if you harbor a terrorist, you're just as guilty as the terrorist.

By the way, when the President of the United States says

---

1. Although the exact reason Flight 93 crashed remains disputed, evidence shows that some of the passengers took control of the plane and stopped the terrorists from crashing it into the White House. The plane crashed in a field near Johnstown, Pennsylvania.   2. Al Qaeda is a terrorist organization believed to be responsible for the terrorist attacks of September 11, 2001.   3. Bush refers to World War II.

something, he better mean it. And when I said to the world, if you harbor a terrorist, you're just as guilty as the terrorist, I meant exactly what I said. And the Taliban found out [when America ousted it in the Fall of 2001]. It wasn't all that long ago that Afghanistan was a training center for al Qaeda killers. It was a safe haven. It's a country, by the way, that was run by a brutal dictatorship. The Taliban had a perverted view of the world. They hated—they must have hated women. Women were given no rights. Young girls did not go to school. There was a barbaric regime. So not only did we uphold doctrine that said, if you harbor a terrorist or train a terrorist or feed a terrorist, you're just as guilty as the terrorist; but we liberated people, as well, in Afghanistan. People are free in that country. Young girls now go to school for the first time in their life, thanks to the incredible compassion of the United States of America.

There's another very important lesson about September the 11th that we must never forget, and that is, we can no longer take threats that may exist overseas for granted. In other words, when the President and/or anybody else in authority sees a threat, we must take it seriously. Now, that doesn't mean every threat must be dealt with by military option, but every threat must be viewed as a potential problem to America. See, September the 11th changed the equation. It used to be that oceans would protect us, that we saw a threat, we didn't have to worry about it because there was two vast oceans. And we could pick and choose as to how we deal with the threat. That changed on September the 11th. . . .

Making America Safer

After September the 11th, we took another vital step to fight terror, and that's what I want to talk about today. I want to talk about the Patriot Act. It's a law that I signed into law. It's a law that was overwhelmingly passed in the House and the Senate. It's a law that is making America safer. It's an important piece of legislation.

First, before September the 11th, law enforcement, intelligence, and national security officials were prevented by legal and bureaucratic restrictions from sharing critical information with each other, and with state and local police departments.

We had—one group of the FBI knows something, but they couldn't talk to the other group in the FBI—because of law and bureaucratic interpretation. You cannot fight the war on terror unless all bodies of your government at the federal, state, and local level are capable of sharing intelligence on a real-time basis. We could not get a complete picture of terrorist threats, therefore. People had—different people had a piece of the puzzle, but because of law, they couldn't get all the pieces in the same piece. And so we removed those barriers, removed the walls. You hear the talk about the walls that separate certain aspects of government; they have been removed by the Patriot Act. And now, law enforcement and intelligence communities are working together to share information to better prevent an attack on America.

And let me give you an interesting story. In late 2001, in Portland, Oregon—and today, I was briefed on this story by the—the federal prosecutor up there, in Oregon—or over there. I'm used to Texas, still. Everything was "up there."

Police in Portland, Oregon turned up evidence about a local man who was planning attacks on Jewish schools and synagogues, and on American troops overseas. The initial information was passed to the FBI and to intelligence services—quickly passed—who analyzed the threat and took action. See, the Patriot Act allowed for unprecedented cooperation. And because of the surveillance tools enacted by the Patriot Act, the FBI learned that this guy was a part of a seven-man terrorist cell. In other words, the Patriot Act gave local—federal law enforcement officials, in this case—the capacity to better understand the intelligence and to better understand the nature of the terrorist cell. And now the cell has been disrupted.

The Tools of the Patriot Act

I'll tell you another good thing that happened. Before September the 11th, investigators had better tools to fight organized crime than to fight international terrorism. That was the reality. For years, law enforcement used so-called roving wire taps to investigate organized crime. You see, what that meant is if you got a wire tap by court order—and, by the way, everything you hear about requires court order, requires there to be permission from a FISA [Foreign Intelligence Surveillance Act] court, for example.

So the crime boss, he'd be on the cell phone, maybe thinking somebody is listening to him, would toss the cell phone and get on another cell phone. And the law allowed for our drug busters to follow the person making the calls, not just a single phone number. So it made it more difficult for a drug lord to evade the net that we were trying to throw on him to capture him with.

Polling the People

Do you think the Bush administration has gone too far, not gone far enough or has been about right in using new laws that give the government more power to fight terrorism?

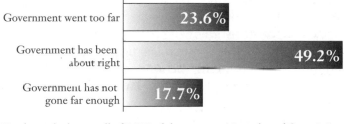

Government went too far	23.6%
Government has been about right	49.2%
Government has not gone far enough	17.7%

Random telephone poll of 1,008 adults over age 18 conducted Sept. 4–8, 2003, for The Associated Press by ICR/International Communications Research.

We couldn't use roving wire taps for terrorists. In other words, terrorists could switch phones and we couldn't follow them. The Patriot Act changed that, and now we have the essential tool. See, with court approval, we have long used roving wire taps to lock up monsters—mobsters. Now we have a chance to lock up monsters, terrorist monsters.

The Patriot Act authorizes what are called delayed notification search warrants. I'm not a lawyer, either. These allow law enforcement personnel, with court approval, to carry out a lawful search without tipping off suspects and giving them a chance to flee or destroy evidence. It is an important part of conducting operations against organized groups.

Before September the 11th, the standards for these kind of warrants were different around the country. It made it hard to have kind of a national strategy to chase down what might be a terrorist group. The Patriot Act provided a clear national standard and now allows these warrants to be used in terrorism cases. And they're an important tool for those who are on the front line of using necessary means, with court order, to find these terrorists before they hurt us. Look, what I'm telling you is, is that the Patriot Act made it easier for people we've tasked to protect America. That's what we want. We want people to have the tools necessary to do the job we expect them to do.

Before September the 11th, law enforcement could more easily obtain business and financial records of white-collar criminals than of suspected terrorists. See, part of the way to make sure that we catch terrorists is we chase money trails. And yet it was easier to chase a money trail with a white-collar criminal than it was a terrorist. The Patriot Act ended this double standard and it made it easier for investigators to catch suspected terrorists by following paper trails here in America.

And finally, before September the 11th, federal judges could often impose tougher prison terms on drug traffickers than they could on terrorists. The Patriot Act strengthened the penalties for crimes committed by terrorists, such as arsons, or attacks on power plants and mass transit systems. In other words, we needed to get—we needed to send the signal, at the very minimum, that our laws are going to be tough on you. When we catch you, you've got a problem, in America. See, that's part of prevention.

Patriot Act Successes

I just outlined five reasons why the Patriot Act made sense. These are practical reasons. These are ways to give our law enforcement officers the tools necessary to do their job so that we can better protect America. And we're making progress.

The last two-and-a-half years, we've dismantled terrorist cells in Oregon and New York and North Carolina and Virginia. We prosecuted terrorist operatives and supportives in California, Ohio, Texas and Florida. In other words, we're using these tools to do the best we can possibly do to protect our fellow citizens. We've frozen or seized about $200 million in terrorist assets around the world. When I say "we" this is now not only United States, but friends and allies.

We're cutting off their money. We're following—what was that movie?—follow the money. That's what we're doing, to make sure that we do our job.

I want you to keep in mind what I've just told you about the Patriot Act the next time you hear somebody attacking the Patriot Act. The Patriot Act defends our liberty. The Patriot Act makes it able for those of us in positions of responsibility to defend the liberty of the American people. It's essential law.

The reason I bring it up is because many of the Patriot Act's anti-terrorism tools are set to expire next year [2004], including key provisions that allow our intelligence and law enforcement agencies to share information. In other words, Congress passed it and said, well, maybe the war on terror won't go on very long, and, therefore, these tools are set to expire. The problem is, the war on terror continues. And yet some senators and congressmen not only want to let the provisions expire, but they want to roll back some of the act's permanent features. And it doesn't make any sense. We can't return to the days of false hope. The terrorists declared war on the United States of America. And the Congress must give law enforcement all the tools necessary to protect the American people.

Expanding the Patriot Act

So I'm starting today to call on the United States Congress to renew the Patriot Act and to make all of its provisions permanent. And not only that, there are some additional things that Congress should do—must do, in my judgment—to strengthen authorities and penalties to defend our homeland. There's something called administrative subpoenas—this is the authority to request certain types of time-sensitive records without the delay of going through a judge or a grand jury. These are critical for many types of investigations. For example, today they're used for health care fraud cases. In other words, those who investigate can use an administrative subpoena to run down somebody cheating the health care system. Yet, in terrorism cases, where speed is of the essence, officials are barred from using administrative subpoenas.

That doesn't seem to make much sense to me. The American people expect us to do our jobs. It seems like we ought to have the very same tool necessary to run down a bad doc as to run down a terrorist. And so when Congress considers the Patriot Act, they ought to be thinking about ways to make sure that we've got the capacity of catching terrorists.

People charged with certain crimes today, including some drug offenses, are eligible for bail only in limited circumstances. But terrorist-related crimes are not on that list. Think about what that means. Suspected terrorists could be released, free to leave the country, or worse, before their trial. And that doesn't make any sense. The disparity makes no sense. If a dangerous drug dealer can be held without bail, the Congress should allow the same treatment for terrorists. If we want to protect our homeland, let's make sure these good people have got the tools necessary to do so.

And there's another example I want to share with you. Under existing law, the death penalty applies to many serious crimes that result in death, including sexual abuse and certain drug-related offenses. Some terrorist crimes that result in death do not qualify for capital punishment. That makes no sense to me. We ought to be sending a strong signal: If you sabotage a defense installation or nuclear facility in a way that takes an innocent life, you ought to get the death penalty, the federal death penalty.

Taking the Offense

The reason why Congress must act is because we have a difficult job protecting America. The reason why is because we're an open society that values freedom. We stand for the—we're a beacon of freedom and we say you can—our country is an open country. And yet that makes us vulnerable—in itself, makes us vulnerable. We got a lot of borders to protect. We got to be right a hundred percent of the time, at the federal level and the state level and the local level. We've got to be right a hundred percent of the time to protect America, and the terrorists have only got to be right one time—as 168 innocent men, women and children found out in [the 1995] Oklahoma City [bombing]. Different forms of terror. We've got to be vigilant against terror at all costs.

And there's only one path to safety and that's the path of action. Congress must act with the Patriot Act. We must continue to stay on the offense when it comes to chasing these killers down and bringing them to justice—and we will. We've got to be strong and resolute and determined. We will never show weakness in the face of these people who have no soul, who have no conscience, who care less about the life of a man or a woman or a child. We've got to do everything we can here at home. And there's no doubt in my mind that, with the Almighty's blessings and hard work, that we will succeed in our mission.

The reason I say that is because I have seen the spirit of this country, I've seen the resolve of our nation. I know the nature of the men and women who proudly call themselves Americans—people who can rise to any challenge; people who are tough; people who are determined; people who are resolute; and people, at the same time, who are compassionate and decent and honorable. And it is my honor to be the President of a country full of such people.

"The public should insist on a full understanding of what the Justice Department is doing before granting the executive branch still more authority."

The Patriot Act Should Not Be Expanded

Anita Ramasastry

In the following viewpoint Anita Ramasastry claims that Patriot II, the Domestic Security Enhancement Act, might expand the police power granted by the Patriot Act. Patriot II, she argues, would make it easier for the government to obtain information on American citizens who have no connection to terrorism. Moreover, Ramasastry asserts, Patriot II increases government secrecy about its spying activities and makes the government immune from liability if it spies illegally. Ramasastry, a law professor at the University of Washington in Seattle, is associate director of the Shidler Center for Law, Commerce & Technology.

As you read, consider the following questions:

1. In Ramasastry's opinion, what type of information would be put into a "Terrorist Identification Database" if Patriot II were passed?
2. What could happen under Patriot II if people try to protect their e-mail from surveillance, in the author's view?
3. According to the author, what important check did the original Patriot Act have that Patriot II does not?

Anita Ramasastry, "Patriot II: The Sequel, Why It's Even Scarier than the First Patriot Act," *Findlaw's Writ*, February 17, 2003. Copyright © 2003 by FindLaw, a Thomson business. This column originally appeared on FindLaw.com. Reproduced by permission.

S oon after the terrorist acts of September 11, [2001] Congress passed the USA Patriot Act, which conferred broad new powers upon the federal government. Now [Attorney General] John Ashcroft and his scribes at the Justice Department have been working secretly to create new, 120-page draft legislation that, if enacted, would expand greatly upon these already sweeping powers.

This daring sequel to the USA Patriot Act is known internally as the Domestic Security Enhancement Act.[1] It is also nicknamed Patriot II (the name by which I'll refer to it here), or Son of Patriot. On February 7 [2003] of this year, a January 9 draft of Patriot II was revealed to the public—but not by the government. It was made public only through a leak.

Even Congress itself, strikingly, appears to have played little or no part in Patriot II's drafting (though it seems that Speaker of the House [Dennis] Hastert was, at least, given the opportunity to review the draft . . . , as was Vice President [Dick] Cheney.)

Perhaps the Bush Administration is looking to repeat its experience with the original USA Patriot Act. Amidst the emotional turmoil after September 11, the Administration introduced the Act and got it enacted in a matter of weeks. The Senate Judiciary Committee had only a brief, one-and-a-half-hour hearing on the Act, in which Attorney General Ashcroft testified but took no questions. In the House, meanwhile, there was no testimony from opponents of the bill.

After September 11, there was at least some rationale for this expedited consideration. Now, however, there is far less exigency. If the introduction of Patriot II in Congress coincides with the Iraq war,[2] it may well be because the Administration has planned it that way, to take advantage of circumstances to ram the bill through both Houses quickly.

Even if Patriot II does end up being introduced in wartime, citizens and their representatives should fight this

---

1. Patriot II has not been officially introduced in either house of Congress and has no official standing. Some claim, however, that portions of the drafted bill have been attached to other bills.   2. Forces primarily from the United States and Great Britain invaded Iraq on March 19, 2003, to depose Iraqi leader Saddam Hussein, whom they accused of supporting terrorists.

legislation tooth and nail, for it threatens to take even more of our liberties away. It is a wholesale assault on privacy, free speech, and freedom of information.

Making Total Information Awareness the Law

Admiral [John] Poindexter's proposed Total Information Awareness (TIA) program, which sought to build data profiles of all Americans, sparked a wide public outcry. Congress . . . warned against using TIA as a tool against US citizens. Nevertheless, Patriot II, as draft by the Attorney General and his staff, would begin to make TIA the law.

For instance, under Patriot II, federal agents would not need a subpoena or obtain a court order to access our consumer credit reports. This provision would open the wedge for TIA to be implemented through a huge database. Our credit reports are repositories of a great deal of sensitive information—from our employment history to where we shop, borrow and transact.

To see the information, the feds would only have to certify that they will use the information "in connection with their duties to enforce federal law." Note that they would *not* have to certify that the person whose information was accessed was suspected of terrorism, *or indeed, any other crime.* And no one would be notified that their records had been accessed. When a commercial entity requests a consumer's credit report, a note is made in the consumer's file alerting him to this fact.

A Mandate to Collect Genetic Information

Meanwhile, not only data, but genetic information would also be collected by the government if Patriot II were passed.

DNA would be put into a "Terrorist Identification Database." It would contain information not only for proven terrorists, but also "suspected terrorists." And that term would include anyone who was associated with, or had provided money or other support for, groups designated "terrorist."

It might also include protesters, or anyone else the government dislikes. Remember, the original USA Patriot Act defined the new crime of "domestic terrorism" broadly, to encompass "any action that endangers human life that is a violation of any Federal or State law."

Certainly one could envision a disruptive war protester who resisted arrest being tagged as a "suspected domestic terrorist," and forced to provide DNA. Would the government need to get a court order to procure the DNA? Not under Patriot II.

And what if the protester wouldn't comply? That would be a Class A misdemeanor, punishable by up to one year in prison and a $100,000 fine. Anyway, the protester's refusing to give up DNA might be futile—if any other government agency happens to have a blood sample, Patriot II gives the government the right to put it in the new database.

Incredibly, DNA would also be collected from anyone who is, or has been, on probation for *any* crime, *no matter how minor.* State governments would be required to collect DNA samples from state probationers and provide them to the federal government.

Increasing Surveillance Powers

Database surveillance, under Patriot II, would also be combined with increased active surveillance of citizens.

To assess the change, it's important to remember that the Patriot Act itself already greatly expanded surveillance powers. Now Patriot II would, if enacted, make it even easier for the government to engage in surveillance of U.S. citizens, without having to establish traditional probable cause under the Fourth Amendment. It would do so by making it easier for law enforcement to avail itself of the Foreign Intelligence Surveillance [FISA] Court, which issues warrants more easily than federal district courts will.

The FISA Court is meant to address international terrorism, involving mostly noncitizens. Patriot II, however collapses the distinction between domestic and international terrorism, treating wholly domestic criminal acts as subject to the same, looser legal rules that apply to foreign intelligence gathering.

Remember, domestic terrorism is defined very broadly as "any action that endangers human life that is a violation of any Federal or State law." That means anything from getting into a raucous bar fight, to driving recklessly over the state speed limit, could theoretically count. And if the government finds a particular person suspicious, they could cite law violations as far from terrorism as these as a valid excuse for surveillance.

Back to Spying on Americans

Section 312 [of the Domestic Security Enhancement Act (DSEA), or, Patriot II] removes checks on local police spying—checks which are designed to prevent . . . governmental persecution based on political and religious activity. Prior to the institution of these checks in the late 1970s, police departments in many cities spied on innocent members of the public who were active in churches, community groups and political organizations. Federal courts, responding to civil rights lawsuits urging an end to such spying, issued decrees prohibiting this spying absent some reason to believe those individuals were involved in criminal or terrorist activity.

The DSEA ends these decrees. . . . Eliminating these sensible, court-approved limits on local police spying would chill dissent, making Americans afraid to join protest groups and activist organizations, attend rallies, or express their views on controversial policies such as abortion or the war in Iraq.

Furthermore, loosening sensible protections on police monitoring of political and religious activity will not make us safer from terrorism. During the years the FBI illegally spied on individuals exercising their rights under the First Amendment, including such civil rights leaders as Dr. Martin Luther King, Jr., resources were diverted and not a single instance of violence was prevented. Freeing local police to spy on innocent individuals is not likely to be any more productive. It only makes us less safe as resources are diverted from more productive investigations, and less free, as individuals find themselves entered into a police database for activities that are constitutionally protected.

Elizabeth Haddix, National Lawyers Guild, March 3, 2003.

Worse, even those persons who cannot be deemed "domestic terrorists" because they have not broken any law, can alternatively be deemed "foreign powers" under Patriot II—*even if they are American citizens or permanent residents.* This allows the FBI to get pen registers on American citizens for a foreign intelligence investigation—without having to show any criminal or terrorist connection.

Gagging American Citizens

If you don't like the government's policies, including these, Patriot II says: Too bad. Don't try to make a federal case out of it—we'll bar you at the courthouse door.

What if you're lucky enough to discover that you've been illegally spied on, in violation of your Fourth Amendment rights? Too bad. Patriot II would provide immunity from liability to law enforcement engaging in spying operations against the American people. The proposed act provides a defense for federal agents who engage unauthorized searches and surveillances relating to foreign intelligence when they are acting "pursuant to a lawful authorization from the President or the Attorney General."

What if a disgruntled business competitor chooses to falsely claim to the government that you're a "suspected terrorist"? Again, too bad. Don't consider suing the competitor, no matter what consequences ensure Patriot II eliminates civil liability for businesses and employees that report "suspected terrorists" to the federal government, no matter how malicious or unfounded the tip may be.

Like TIA, Operation TIPS [Terrorism Information and Prevention System]—which would have enlisted government employees to spy on citizens—elicited public outcry. But this is TIPS all over again. If they like, your package courier or cable guy can report you to the feds with impunity.

Broadly Criminalizing Encryption of Evidence

Meanwhile, in your search for a shred of privacy that might remain to you, don't even think about trying to protect your email. Under Patriot II, the government may go after you for that, too.

Specifically, Patriot II, as currently drafted, would make it a new, separate crime to use encryption in the commission of another crime. To be convicted, the defendant must be shown to have "knowingly and willfully use[d] encryption technology to conceal any incriminating communication" relating to a federal felony he is committing, or attempting to commit.

The "federal crime" limitation may seem significant, until you realize that "domestic terrorism"—which can be based

143

on a state law violation—is a federal crime. Remember, too, how loosely "domestic terrorism" is defined, in a way that could encompass a protester's resisting arrest, and if you do, you may reasonably fear using encryption even if you are not engaged in any criminal activity at all.

What if your encrypted email about protest planning is deemed "incriminating evidence" of your plan to resist arrest at the protest? You could be looking at five to ten.

The penalty for this offense alone would be up to ten years in prison. In addition, a Justice Department analysis included with the proposal suggests that the illegal encrypting ought to carry a mandatory minimum term of five years in prison.

Notably, the federal felony relating to the "incriminating communication" *need not be an act of terrorism.* It could be *any* federal crime, from the most major to the most minor, the most violent to the most excruciatingly technical. And that's frightening.

For instance, if a peer-to-peer website's users swap files, thus violating the Digital Millennium Copyright Act, and encrypt the files they are swapping, they may automatically face five years in prison, and could serve ten, for the encryption alone.

What is most shocking about the new encryption crime is that it is not limited to terrorism. This is the first attempt to regulate encryption domestically at all.

Shrouding Government Actions in Secrecy

While the government, according to Patriot II, has the right to know virtually everything about you, you have little right to know anything about the government.

Current grand jury secrecy rules apply only to jurors, prosecutors and courtroom staff. Patriot II would expand them to apply to witnesses too—meaning that ordinary citizens could not discuss their testimony with anyone but their attorney. In theory, they'd have to keep mum even with spouses or children, or face serious consequences.

What if they've been improperly subpoenaed in the first place? Under Patriot II, too bad: Neither individuals nor organizations may move to try to quash a federal grand jury subpoena.

Will the grand jury itself at least remain independent? Nope. Patriot II allows the federal government to place gag orders on both federal and state grand juries, and to take over the proceedings.

Detentions will be similarly shrouded in an atmosphere of dead secrecy. The Justice Department's position on detainees is that if they are held incommunicado indefinitely without being charged with a crime, they need not be publicly identified. Patriot II would make that dubious position the law.

Meanwhile, if you do happen to somehow find out the identity or whereabouts of—or anything else about—a detainee, it would be criminal under Patriot II to reveal it. And that's the case even if you are the detainee's parent, spouse, or child.

Okay, you might ask, this is a lot of secrecy, but isn't it at least somewhat limited? Can't I at least use the Freedom of Information Act (FOIA) to figure out what the government is doing when it's *not* secretly detaining people, or secretly conducting grand jury proceedings?

No. Under Patriot II, FOIA would not extend to information "specifically exempted from disclosure by statute." What kind of statutes? Well, the USA Patriot Act might be one. Patriot II might be another.

It's a clever strategy: Collect private information. And then when citizens try to find out what you've collected, cite their own privacy right back at them as a reason not to divulge it.

If it seems farfetched to think the government could invoke privacy in this instance, consider that Ashcroft actually cited detainees' privacy as a reason not to release their names to the press, the public, or even their families.

The Citizenship Death Penalty

In sum, Patriot II puts in jeopardy the First Amendment right to speak freely, statutory and common law rights to privacy, the right to go to court to challenge government illegality, and the Fourth Amendment right against unreasonable searches and seizures. But that's not all.

It also puts in jeopardy perhaps the most basic right of all:

145

The right to walk the streets in safety without being "disappeared" by the government. Chileans have not always enjoyed this right. Americans, until now, always have.

Suppose you, as a citizen, attended a legal protest for which one of the hosts, unbeknownst to you, is an organization the government has listed as terrorist. Under Patriot II, you may be deported and deemed no longer an American citizen.

Under Patriot II, if you are simply *suspected* of terrorist activity, this can occur. More specifically, a U.S. citizen may be expatriated "if, with the intent to relinquish his nationality, he becomes a member of, or provides material support to, a group that the United States has designated as a 'terrorist organization.'"

How can you tell if the citizen wanted to relinquish citizenship? Under Patriot II, the intent can be inferred from conduct. So any association with even the legal activities of a designated group, plus any act that can be interpreted as disloyal to the United States, can mean you are deported, and no longer considered a citizen.

No Sunset Provisions for Patriot II

The original USA Patriot Act has sunset provisions, under which the Act will expire if not renewed in five years. Patriot II, however, does not have such provisions. Indeed, it would go so far as to remove this important check from the original Patriot Act. So if Congress, and the American people don't focus carefully on Patriot II, even in the midst of impending war, we may be stuck with both Patriot Acts indefinitely.

Especially for that reason, Congress and the public need to learn more. Senator Patrick Leahy has argued, for instance, that before the Department of Justice asks Congress for more powers, it needs to disclose how it is using the ones it already has. Instead, the Department has so far repeatedly balked at both FOIA requests from the press and the public and requests from Congress for more detailed reporting pursuant to USA Patriot Act.

At the very least, Congress and the public should insist on a full understanding of what the Justice Department is doing before granting the executive branch still more authority via Patriot II.

"Sunset [provisions] will allow Congress to make some needed adjustments . . . and strengthen the protections for civil liberties without sacrificing security."

The Patriot Act Should Be Amended

John Podesta

Although an effective tool to track terrorists, the Patriot Act must be amended to better protect civil liberties, argues John Podesta in the following viewpoint. The act applies laws that govern telephone surveillance to Internet surveillance, for example, which could lead to abuse, Podesta asserts. Moreover, the Patriot Act also loosens the requirements for obtaining foreign and domestic intelligence, which could lead to spying on American citizens who are not terrorists. Therefore, he contends, the act should be amended to increase judicial oversight of surveillance activities. Podesta, former U.S. president Bill Clinton's Chief of Staff, is professor of law at Georgetown University in Washington, D.C.

As you read, consider the following questions:
1. Why can the government learn a tremendous amount of information about a person, in Podesta's view?
2. According to the author, how could amending section 206 of the Patriot Act prevent abuse of roaming wiretaps?
3. In the author's opinion, what gave rise to the original opposition to the Patriot Act?

John Podesta, "USA Patriot Act: The Good, the Bad, and the Sunset," *Human Rights*, vol. 29, Winter 2002. Copyright © 2003 by the American Bar Association. Reproduced by permission.

R ecent tragic events [the terrorist attacks of September 11, 2001] have brought about a rapid reconsideration of the legal restrictions placed on law enforcement and the intelligence communities. On October 26, [2001] President [George W.] Bush signed into law the USA Patriot Act (Patriot Act), which makes significant changes in the legal structure within which the law enforcement and intelligence communities operate. This article focuses on the key provisions of the Patriot Act that pertain to electronic surveillance and intelligence gathering. Notwithstanding the haste with which Congress acted, the provisions of the new law relating to electronic surveillance, for the most part, are a sound effort to provide new tools for law enforcement and intelligence agencies to combat terrorism while preserving the civil liberties of individual Americans. Some changes simply update our surveillance laws to reflect the fact that we live in a digital age. Other sections expand the surveillance powers of our law enforcement and intelligence communities in ways that make sense in light of the new threats facing our country.

When we decide, however, to expand surveillance powers to track terrorists, *all* residents, not just the terrorists, are affected. A common problem running through many of the new authorities contained in the Patriot Act is the reliance on executive branch supervision rather than meaningful review by a neutral magistrate of the potentially highly intrusive surveillance techniques that are authorized. There are several common sense changes that could be made to the new law that would provide better protections for civil liberties without sacrificing security. Because of the rapidity with which the law was enacted, Congress, wisely, included a four-year sunset of many of the provisions of the new Act. That sunset will allow Congress to make some needed adjustments, hopefully in a calmer climate, and strengthen the protections for civil liberties without sacrificing security.

Accessing Computer Information

The Patriot Act substantially changes the law with respect to law enforcement access to information about computer use including Web surfing. Reaching for an analogy from the old rotary dialed telephone system, the Act extends provisions written to authorize installation of pen registers and trap and trace devices, which record outgoing and incoming phone numbers, to authorize the installation of devices to record all computer routing, addressing, and signaling information. The government can get this information with a mere certification that the information likely to be obtained is relevant to an ongoing criminal investigation.

Today, with more than fifty million U.S. households online, when more than 1.4 billion e-mails change hands every day, when computer users surf the Web and download files using phone lines, mobile devices, and cable modems, the government can learn a tremendous amount of information about you from where you shop to what you read to who your friends are through the use of so-called transactional records. The potential for abuse, for invasion of privacy, and for profiling citizens is high. That's why it is disappointing that the authors of this provision settled for an incredibly weak standard of judicial oversight. A better analogy might have been to the provision of the Electronic Communications Privacy Act governing access to the stored records of Internet service providers, which permits a judge to satisfy herself that there are specific and articulable facts that the information sought is relevant and material to the ongoing investigation. This is a provision that Congress should review as part of its sunset process and amend.

Collecting Information on American Citizens

Previously, domestic law enforcement and foreign intelligence collection operated on separate tracks. This separation was seen as necessary because of the very different legal regimes that are associated with domestic law enforcement and foreign intelligence collection. The events of September 11, which involved several individuals who had lived in our country for some time, made it clear that more cooperation between domestic law enforcement and foreign intelligence collection was necessary. Section 203 facilitates this cooperation by allowing "foreign intelligence information" gathered in criminal investigations by domestic law enforcement to be shared with the intelligence community. In this manner, section 203 enables the intelligence community access to critical information that might otherwise be unavailable.

The definition of "foreign intelligence information" contained in the Patriot Act is quite broad. Foreign intelligence is defined to mean "information relating to the capabilities, intentions, or activities of foreign governments or elements thereof, foreign organizations, or foreign persons or international terrorist activities." The definition goes on to specifically include information about a U.S. person that concerns a foreign power or foreign territory and "relates to the national defense or the security of the United States" or "the conduct of the foreign affairs of the United States." The sharing of such a broad range of information raises the specter of intelligence agencies, once again, collecting, profiling, and potentially harassing U.S. persons engaged in lawful, First Amendment-protected activities.

Section 203 provides some protection against abuse by requiring that when information originates from grand juries or wiretaps, the attorney general must establish procedures for the disclosure of "foreign intelligence information" that identifies a U.S. person. These safeguards need to be strengthened in two regards. First, to prevent unnecessary dissemination of information about a U.S. person to the intelligence community, such procedures should also be required for information obtained in domestic criminal investigations generally. Second, information subject to grand jury secrecy rules should only be disseminated with authorization from a court.

Controlling Wiretaps

The Foreign Intelligence Surveillance Act (FISA) facilitates domestic intelligence gathering related to foreign powers by allowing the collection of such information without the legal restrictions associated with domestic law enforcement. Section 206 of the Patriot Act modernizes FISA wiretap authority. Previously, FISA required a separate court order be obtained for each communication carrier used by the target of an investigation. In the era of cell phones, pay phones, e-mail, instant messaging, and BlackBerry wireless e-mail devices such a requirement is a significant barrier in monitoring an individual's communications. Section 206 allows a single wiretap to legally "roam" from device to device, to tap the person rather than the phone. In 1986, Congress authorized the use of roaming wiretaps in criminal investigations that are generally subject to stricter standards than FISA intelligence gathering, so extending this authority to FISA was a natural step.

The main difference between roaming wiretaps under current criminal law and the new FISA authority is that current criminal law requires that law enforcement "ascertain" that the target of a wiretap is actually using a device to be tapped. Section 206 contains no such provision. Ensuring that FISA wiretaps only roam when intelligence officials "ascertain" that the subject of an investigation is using a device, before it is tapped, would prevent abuse of this provision. For example, without the ascertainment requirement, it is conceivable that all the pay phones in an entire neighborhood could be tapped if suspected terrorists happened to be in that neighborhood. Bringing FISA roaming wiretaps in line with criminal roaming wiretaps would prevent such abuse and provide greater protection to the privacy of ordinary Americans.

Monitoring Searches

The 1986 Electronic Communications Privacy Act granted the government the authority to delay notification for search of some forms of electronic communications that are in the custody of a third party. Section 213 statutorily extends the ability of law enforcement to delay the notice to any physical or electronic search with a showing that notice would create an "adverse result." This provision is an effort to improve the government's ability to investigate suspected terrorists by granting law enforcement greater leeway to operate clandestinely. To a large extent, section 213 simply codifies existing law enforcement practice in a manner consistent with recent court decisions. Nevertheless, the "adverse result" standard (defined in 18 U.S.C. § 2705), by virtue of its ambiguity, creates the potential for abuse. As a result, section 213, which is not currently subject to the four-year sunset contained in the Act, should, nevertheless, be carefully reviewed at that time.

If someone unlawfully enters your home, you can ask the

police to enter your premise without a warrant to investigate. Section 217 clarifies that similar authority applies to "computer trespassers." This allows law enforcement, with the permission of the owner of a computer, to monitor a trespasser's action without obtaining an order for a wiretap. This provision constrains the ability of hackers to use computers without being detected.

Looking for Limits on Police Power

In the debate over the PATRIOT Act, civil libertarians did not argue that the government should be denied the tools it needs to monitor terrorists' communications or otherwise carry out effective investigations. Instead, privacy advocates urged that those powers be focused and subject to clear standards and judicial review. The tragedy of the response to September 11 is not that the government has been given new powers—it is that those new powers have been granted without standards or checks and balances.

We need limits on government surveillance and guidelines for the use of information not merely to protect individual rights but to focus government activity on those planning violence. The criminal standard and the principle of particularized suspicion keep the government from being diverted into investigations guided by politics, religion or ethnicity. Meaningful judicial controls do not tie the government's hands—they ensure that the guilty are identified and that the innocent are promptly exonerated.

James X. Dempsey, Center for Democracy & Technology, testimony before the Senate Committee on the Judiciary, November 18, 2003.

Although most law-abiding computer users' online activities will not be monitored by the government as a result of section 217, the new authority may be overbroad. A "computer trespasser" is defined as anyone who accesses a protected computer (which includes any computer connected to the Internet) without authorization. Individuals who exceed their terms of service agreements with their Internet service provider or individuals who use their computer at work to download an MP3 file could be subject to intrusive government monitoring. While the need to respond quickly to malicious hacking, such as denial of service attacks, provides a basis for this provision, section 217 should be amended to require court authorization for monitoring of individual users that exceeds forty-eight hours in duration.

Spying on Americans

Prior to the enactment of FISA in 1978, the intelligence community had virtually unchecked authority to conduct domestic surveillance of U.S. citizens and organizations. FISA created a special court to ensure that "the purpose" of domestic intelligence gathering was to obtain foreign intelligence information. The FISA court structure and sole purpose standard attempted to balance the need to collect foreign intelligence information without the constraints of the Fourth Amendment with increased protections for Americans exercising their First Amendment rights. But the sole purpose test has created operational difficulties for foreign intelligence investigations that uncover criminal wrongdoing and lead to an investigation of the criminal conduct. The events of September 11 further blur the line between foreign intelligence investigation and domestic law enforcement and the ability to jointly work the case and share information between the intelligence and law enforcement communities has become more important in the context of the investigations of Al Qaeda [the terrorist group responsible for the September 11 attacks]. Section 218 loosens the standard of a FISA investigation by requiring a showing that the collection of foreign intelligence information is "a significant purpose" rather than "the purpose" of an investigation. Section 218 is an important tool for counterterrorism but, since probable cause is not required under FISA, it also raises the possibility that U.S. citizens who are not terrorists could have their homes searched and communications monitored without probable cause. Therefore, section 218 deserves special attention when it expires. . . .

Many of the electronic surveillance provisions in the Patriot Act faced serious opposition prior to September 11 from a coalition of privacy advocates, computer users, and elements of high-tech industry. The events of September 11 convinced many in that coalition and overwhelming majorities in Congress that law enforcement and national security officials need new legal tools to fight terrorism. But we should not forget what gave rise to the original opposition—many aspects of the bill increase the opportunity for law enforcement and the intelligence community to return to an era where they monitored and sometimes harassed individuals who were merely exercising their First Amendment rights. Nothing that occurred on September 11 mandates that we return to such an era. If anything, the events of September 11 should redouble our resolve to protect the rights we as Americans cherish. Therefore, as the new powers granted under the Patriot Act begin to be exercised, we should not only feel more confident that our country has the tools to be safe but we should be ever vigilant that these new tools are not abused.

| *"Congress initially sunset the Patriot Act to terminate after a five-year period for the simple reason that it was only seen as an emergency measure."* |

The Patriot Act Should Be Terminated

John W. Whitehead

In the following viewpoint constitutional law attorney John W. Whitehead explains that the Patriot Act is an emergency measure passed after the terrorist attacks of September 11, 2001, with a built-in five-year life span. He argues that the act should be allowed to expire in 2005, as it severely curtails civil liberties: it inhibits free expression, violates privacy, and allows intrusive searches and seizures without judicial oversight. Whitehead is president of the Rutherford Institute, a civil liberties organization.

As you read, consider the following questions:
1. In Whitehead's opinion, how have some 34 million Americans reacted to the Patriot Act?
2. According to the author, what are "black bag" and "sneak and peak" searches?
3. How does the Patriot Act emasculate the Bill of Rights, in the author's view?

John W. Whitehead, "The President Is Wrong: The USA Patriot Act Should Be Terminated," www.rutherford.org, January 26, 2004. Copyright © 2004 by the Rutherford Institute. Reproduced by permission.

A mere 45 days after the September 11th [2001] terrorist attacks, President [George W.] Bush signed into law the USA Patriot Act. A politician's dream—and a civil libertarian's nightmare—the Patriot Act broadened the already immense powers of the federal government, not only in regard to investigations relating to terrorism but also to criminal investigations. At some 342 pages, this massive, complex, highly technical 30,000-word statute is divided into ten titles, with more than 270 sections and endless subsections that cross-reference and amend a dozen or more different laws. Most of our congressional representatives admitted that they did not even read this monstrosity before they voted to pass it. Hidden within this tome are provisions that turn the FBI, CIA and INS, [Immigration and Naturalization Service] into secret police.

Many Americans have reacted negatively to the Patriot Act's Orwellian nature. Indeed, 234 cities, towns and counties have . . . passed resolutions, ordinances or ballot initiatives prohibiting their local police from complying with the Patriot Act. These people represent an aggregate of some 34 million Americans.

Thus, it was with some surprise that President Bush in his [2004] State of the Union speech aggressively endorsed the Patriot Act as "one of those essential tools" in the so-called war against terrorism. Without citing a shred of evidence that the Patriot Act has been effective in fighting terrorism, the President asked Congress to extend its term, which is set to expire [in 2005]. Congress initially sunset the Patriot Act to terminate after a five-year period for the simple reason that it was only seen as an emergency measure.

Reasons for Alarm

Why all the concern about the Patriot Act by millions of Americans? Here are a few, among many, reasons for alarm.

Under the Patriot Act, the definition of terrorism is expanded to cover anyone or any group that tries to bring about change for political or ideological reasons and uses any kind of force to bring it about. This could range from nailing a poster to a courthouse door to carrying a picket sign. Thus, the government now has the authority to harass a broad range of political dissenters, ranging from Greenpeace to anti-abortion protesters to environmental activists to the National Rifle Association.

Under the Patriot Act, the government can, and most likely already has, conducted black bag and sneak and peak searches. In other words, government agents—much like other authoritarian regimes—can now enter your apartment or home and look through your documents, computer files and possessions ("sneak and peak") or take documents, files and possessions ("black bag") without giving you notice that they've ever been on your property.

American Citizens Deserve Better

The law is murky; and the [Patriot Act] passed in the aftermath of [the terrorist attacks of September 11, 2001] adds new elements of uncertainty. Nonetheless, the controlling principle is unambiguous. Any attempt by government to chip away at constitutionally guaranteed rights must be subjected to the most painstaking scrutiny to determine whether less invasive means could accomplish the same ends. The USA-PATRIOT anti-terrorism bill does not survive that demanding test. In a free society, we deserve better.

Robert A. Levy, *Cato Institute*, 2001. www.cato.org/current/terrorism/pubs/levy-martial-law.html.

Also under the Patriot Act, the government has routine access to your educational and financial/banking records as long as the government asserts that snooping through your records is "related to a terrorism investigation." What this means is that all a government agent has to say to get access to your records is, "We're conducting a terrorism investigation." And, believe it or not, your school or bank cannot inform you that the government has gotten this information.

The Patriot Act allows government agents to conduct document searches and seizures of businesses as well. Moreover, any company, including employers, libraries, Internet providers, banks, bookstores and video stores must provide all records relating to the subject under investigation. Again, these entities cannot inform anyone, including the suspect or the media, that they have been rifling through their files.

A violation of this provision is a federal offense that can result in imprisonment.

Under the Patriot Act, the government is allowed to conduct roving wiretaps. Any judge can issue a wiretap order for a telephone line, Internet line or e-mail system anywhere in the U.S. in order to follow a targeted individual anywhere—even if the individual is not named by the government. Known as a "Doe" target, it means that if you are labeled a suspected terrorist, any of your electronic communications are continually monitored by the government. This obviously makes it easier for the FBI—using the powerful Internet spying technology called Carnivore—to monitor computers, read e-mails and track which web pages are visited by American citizens with merely the say-so of an employer or university.

Emasculating the Bill of Rights

There are many other intrusive and violative provisions of the Patriot Act, which clearly and dramatically emasculates key provisions of our Bill of Rights. Not only does it inhibit and chill free expression by American citizens, it is also an intrusive violation of our privacy and undermines the Fourth Amendment to our Constitution, which protects against unreasonable searches and seizures. There was obviously some concern about this by Congress, which is the reason that the Patriot Act was sunset at five years.

One day after the terrorist attacks on the World Trade Center and the Pentagon traumatized our nation, President Bush vowed, "We will not allow this enemy to win the war by changing our way of life or restricting our freedoms." Unfortunately, by becoming an aggressive advocate of the Patriot Act, the President is doing just that.

During Bush's State of the Union speech, he emphasized that a key role of our government was to protect us from foreign terrorists. However, if the Bush Administration continues to advocate such measures as the Patriot Act, then an important question is raised: Who will protect us from our own government?

*"The [True Patriot Act] would make 11
sections of the Patriot Act null and void."*

Unconstitutional Sections of the Patriot Act Should Be Repealed

Charles Levendosky

Some provisions of the Patriot Act violate the U.S. Constitution and should be repealed, argues Charles Levendosky in the following viewpoint. A new version of the act, called the Benjamin Franklin True Patriot Act, would remove eleven sections of the Patriot Act that sacrifice Americans' civil liberties. In Levendosky's opinion, the most offending provisions include delayed notification searches, warrantless searches of library and financial records, and the act's use of overly-broad definitions of domestic terrorism. Levendosky, creator of the First Amendment Cyber-Tribune (FACT) and defender of civil liberties, died March 14, 2004.

As you read, consider the following questions:

1. According to Levendosky, what was the effect of broader application of the Foreign Intelligence Surveillance Act authorized by the Patriot Act, Section 218?
2. What examples does the author give to show that the True Patriot Act would roll back federal government policing powers?
3. In the author's view, what will passage of the True Patriot Act tell the Bush administration about the American people?

The backlash against the USA PATRIOT Act of 2001 is picking up speed and snap.

On Sept. 24, [2003] Democratic presidential candidate Rep. Dennis Kucinich of Ohio and Texas Republican Rep. Ron Paul introduced the Benjamin Franklin True Patriot Act (H.R. 3171)[1] to repeal the most controversial sections of the Patriot Act as well as some of the more egregious actions taken by the Department of Justice.

When introducing the True Patriot Act, Kucinich told members of the House: "Twenty-four months after the September 11th [2001] attacks, this nation has undergone a dramatic political change, leading to an unprecedented assault on the United States Constitution and the Bill of Rights."

The act already has 20 other co-sponsors, at this point all Democrats, but as the word gets out concerning key elements of this bill, expect conservatives, moderates and liberals to push for its passage.

The Kucinich-Paul bill has already garnered the support of the American Civil Liberties Union, National Association for the Advancement of Colored People (NAACP), American Muslim Voice, Council on American Islamic Relations (CAIR), and Religious Action Center of Reformed Judaism.

The True Patriot Act

The True Patriot Act heralds its intent by quoting Benjamin Franklin's famous statement: "Those who would give up essential Liberty, to purchase a little temporary Safety, deserve neither Liberty or Safety."

The act would make 11 sections of the Patriot Act null and void 90 days after the bill is enacted. Under the language of the bill, the president can request Congress to hold hearings to determine whether a particular section should be removed from the repeal list prior to the end of the 90-day period. Congress may or may not honor that request.

The True Patriot Act would repeal Section 213 of the Patriot Act which authorized property to be searched and

1. As of this writing the bill remains in the following House committees, in each case for consideration of such provisions as fall within the jurisdiction of the committee concerned: the Judiciary, Intelligence (Permanent Select), Education and the Workforce, Government Reform, and Transportation and Infrastructure.

seized in secret by government law enforcement officials, without notifying the subject of a warrant.

The act would repeal Section 214 and Section 216, relating to the use of pen registers for foreign intelligence purposes and criminal cases. Pen registers record all phone numbers dialed from a person's telephone.

It would repeal Section 215 which authorized searches of library, bookstore, medical, financial, religious and travel records without a judicial warrant.

Wasserman. © 2003 by *Liberal Opinion Week*. Reproduced by permission of Knight-Ridder/Tribune Information Services.

The True Patriot Act repeals the broader application of the Foreign Intelligence Surveillance Act authorized by the Patriot Act, Section 218. This section of the Patriot Act, in essence, gutted the Fourth Amendment's requirement for probable cause to obtain a search warrant in criminal investigations.

The act repeals Sections 411 and 412 of the Patriot Act which granted new grounds for the deportation and/or the mandatory detention of aliens.

The act also repeals Section 505 of the Patriot Act which authorized FBI field agents to issue national security letters to obtain financial, bank and credit records of individuals—all without a court order or judicial oversight.

And the True Patriot Act repeals Sections 507 and 508 of the Patriot Act relating to the seizure of educational records and the disclosure of individually identifiable information under the National Education Statistics Act of 1994.

Finally, in regard to the Patriot Act, the True Patriot Act repeals Section 802 which defined the new crime of "domestic terrorism." The definition is so broad political protests that unaccountably become violent could be classified as domestic terrorism.

The Benjamin Franklin True Patriot Act also repeals sections of the Homeland Security Act of 2002, so that the Department of Justice and the Department of Homeland Security are no longer exempt from Freedom of Information Act (FOIA) requests.

Reigning in Police Powers

The True Patriot Act goes further—to roll back policing powers the federal government took upon itself since Sept. 11, without congressional authorization.

For instance, the federal government would no longer be able to monitor conversations between attorneys and their clients, violating the fundamental right of attorney-client privilege.

The act would void U.S. Attorney General John Ashcroft's memorandum to all agencies of the federal government narrowing the scope of FOIA and the ability of citizens to obtain information about how their government is working.

The act reinstates tough guidelines instituted in 1989 by former Attorney General Dick Thornburg to rein in a runaway FBI that had been conducting unlawful surveillance of protesters, peace demonstrators and religious groups. Spying on religious institutions—allowed by Ashcroft's rules—would be put under strict limits.

The True Patriot Act repeals special immigration detention regulations and policies instituted after Sept. 11. Immigration hearings would no longer be closed under the act, unless there were special circumstances. Immigration or Justice Department officials would no longer be able to hold non-citizens for indefinite periods of time without charges being filed. The federal regulation which requires all male immigrants from Arab or Muslim countries to register with their local immigration officials would be repealed by the act.

The Patriot Act of 2001, a 342-page document, was passed without meaningful review. Many members of Congress hadn't read the bill; some still haven't. The Patriot Act violates the civil liberties and due process rights of American citizens and immigrants.

The Benjamin Franklin True Patriot Act would rectify the Patriot Act's serious short-comings. And, if passed, the True Patriot Act would put this administration on notice that the American people will not barter away their fundamental liberties for so-called safety. Americans understand the risks involved in living with and for freedom—after all, our freedom was born in revolution.

"The most notorious stain on the presidency of John Adams began . . . with the passage of a series of laws startlingly similar to the Patriot Act."

History Shows Why the Patriot Act Should Be Abolished

Thom Hartmann

In the following viewpoint Thom Hartmann argues that the U.S. government should learn the lessons of an earlier Patriot Act. The Alien and Sedition Acts of 1798, claims Hartmann, were remarkably similar to today's Patriot Act; they restricted immigration and allowed the president to detain and deport dangerous aliens and punish political dissenters. As a result, many of Adams' opponents were arrested, Hartmann asserts. The Bush administration should note that the public outrage at these acts ended Adams' presidency, he maintains, and was strikingly similar to the backlash against Bush's Patriot Act. Hartmann, author of *We the People: A Call to Take Back America*, hosts a nationally syndicated daily radio talk show.

As you read, consider the following questions:

1. In Hartmann's opinion, how did John Adams and Thomas Jefferson differ in their response to outspoken newspaper editors?
2. According to the author, what happened to the newspapers of some of the editors arrested as a result of the Alien and Sedition Acts?
3. How does the history of John Adams' failed presidency give hope to those committed to real democracy and genuine freedom, in the author's view?

M any Americans are suggesting that the Patriot Act (and its proposed "improvements" in Patriot II)[1] is totally new in the experience of America and may spell the end of both democracy and the Bill of Rights. History, however, shows another view, which offers us both warnings and hope.

Silencing John Adams' Critics

Although you won't learn much about it from reading the "Republican histories" of the Founders being published and promoted in the corporate media these days, the most notorious stain on the presidency of John Adams began in 1798 with the passage of a series of laws startlingly similar to the Patriot Act.

It started when Benjamin Franklin Bache, grandson of Benjamin Franklin and editor of the Philadelphia newspaper the *Aurora*, began to speak out against the policies of then-President John Adams. Bache supported Vice President Thomas Jefferson's Democratic-Republican Party (today called the Democratic Party) when John Adams led the conservative Federalists (who today would be philosophically identical to GOP Republicans). Bache attacked Adams in an op-ed piece by calling the president "old, querulous, Bald, blind, crippled, Toothless Adams."

To be sure, Bache wasn't the only one attacking Adams in 1798. His *Aurora* was one of about 20 independent newspapers aligned with Jefferson's Democratic-Republicans, and many were openly questioning Adams' policies and ridiculing Adams' fondness for formality and grandeur.

On the Federalist side, conservative newspaper editors were equally outspoken. Noah Webster wrote that Jefferson's Democratic-Republicans were "the refuse, the sweepings of the most depraved part of mankind from the most corrupt nations on each." Another Federalist characterized the Democratic-Republicans as "democrats, momocrats and all other kinds of rats," while Federalist newspapers worked hard to turn the rumor of Jefferson's relationship with his

---

1. The author refers to the Domestic Security Enhancement Act of 2003, which has not been officially introduced in either house of Congress and has no official standing. Some claim, however, that portions of the drafted bill have been attached to other bills.

deceased wife's half-sister, slave Sally Hemmings, into a full-blown scandal.

But while Jefferson and his Democratic-Republicans had learned to develop a thick skin, University of Missouri-Rolla history professor Larry Gragg points out in an October 1998 article in *American History* magazine that Bache's writings sent Adams and his wife into a self-righteous frenzy. Abigail wrote to her husband and others that Benjamin Franklin Bache was expressing the "malice" of a man possessed by Satan. The Democratic-Republican newspaper editors were engaging, she said, in "abuse, deception, and falsehood," and Bache was a "lying wretch."

Abigail insisted that her husband and Congress must act to punish Bache for his "most insolent and abusive" words about her husband and his administration. His "wicked and base, violent and calumniating abuse" must be stopped, she demanded.

Abigail Adams followed the logic employed by modern-day "conservatives" who call the administration "the government" and say that those opposed to an administration's policies are "unpatriotic," by writing that Bache's "abuse" being "leveled against the Government" of the United States (her husband) could even plunge the nation into a "civil war."

The Alien and Sedition Acts

Worked into a frenzy by Abigail Adams and Federalist newspapers of the day, Federalist senators and congressmen—who controlled both legislative houses along with the presidency—came to the defense of John Adams by passing a series of four laws that came to be known together as the Alien and Sedition Acts.

The vote was so narrow—44 to 41 in the House of Representatives—that in order to ensure passage the lawmakers wrote a sunset provision into its most odious parts: Those laws, unless renewed, would expire the last day of John Adams' first term of office, March 3, 1801.

Empowered with this early version of the Patriot Act, President John Adams ordered his "unpatriotic" opponents arrested, and specified that only Federalist judges on the Supreme Court would be both judges and jurors.

Bache, often referred to as "Lightning Rod Junior" after his famous grandfather, was the first to be hauled into jail (before the laws even became effective!), followed by *New York Time Piece* editor John Daly Burk, which put his paper out of business. Bache died of yellow fever while awaiting trial, and Burk accepted deportation to avoid imprisonment and then fled.

Others didn't avoid prison so easily. Editors of seventeen of the twenty or so Democratic-Republican-affiliated newspapers were arrested, and ten were convicted and imprisoned; many of their newspapers went out of business.

Bache's successor, William Duane (who both took over the newspaper and married Bache's widow), continued the attacks on Adams, publishing in the June 24, 1799 issue of the *Aurora* a private letter John Adams had written to Tench Coxe in which then-Vice President Adams admitted that there were still men influenced by Great Britain in the U.S. government. The letter cast Adams in an embarrassing light, as it implied that Adams himself may still have British loyalties (something suspected by many, ever since his pre-revolutionary defense of British soldiers involved in the Boston Massacre), and made the quick-tempered Adams furious.

Planning Secret Elections

Imprisoning his opponents in the press was only the beginning for Adams, though. Knowing Jefferson would mount a challenge to his presidency in 1800, he and the Federalists hatched a plot to pass secret legislation that would have disputed presidential elections decided "in secret" and "behind closed doors."

Duane got evidence of the plot, and published it just after having published the letter that so infuriated Adams. It was altogether too much for the president who didn't want to let go of his power: Adams had Duane arrested and hauled before Congress on Sedition Act charges. Duane would have stayed in jail had not Thomas Jefferson intervened, letting Duane leave to "consult his attorney." Duane went into hiding until the end of the Adams' presidency.

Emboldened, the Federalists reached out beyond just newspaper editors.

When Congress let out in July of 1798, John and Abigail Adams made the trip home to Braintree, Massachusetts in their customary fashion—in fancy carriages as part of a parade, with each city they passed through firing cannons and ringing church bells. (The Federalists were, after all, as Jefferson said, the party of "the rich and the well born." Although Adams wasn't one of the super-rich, he basked in their approval and adopted royal-like trappings, later discarded by Jefferson.)

As the Adams family entourage, full of pomp and ceremony, passed through Newark, New Jersey, a man named Luther Baldwin was sitting in a tavern and probably quite unaware that he was about to make a fateful comment that would help change history.

As Adams rode by, soldiers manning the Newark cannons loudly shouted the Adams-mandated chant, "Behold the chief who now commands!" and fired their salutes. Hearing the cannon fire as Adams drove by outside the bar, in a moment of drunken candor Luther Baldwin said, "There goes the President and they are firing at his arse." Baldwin further compounded his sin by adding that, "I do not care if they fire thro' his arse!"

The tavern's owner, a Federalist named John Burnet, overheard the remark and turned Baldwin in to Adams thought police: The hapless drunk was arrested, convicted, and imprisoned for uttering "seditious words tending to defame the President and Government of the United States."

Tolerating No Opposition

The Alien and Sedition Acts reflected the new attitude Adams and his wife had brought to Washington D.C. in 1796, a take-no-prisoners type of politics in which no opposition was tolerated.

For example, on January 30, 1798, Vermont's Congressman Matthew Lyon spoke out on the floor of the House against "the malign influence of Connecticut politicians." Charging that Adams and the Federalists only served the interests of the rich and had "acted in opposition to the interests and opinions of nine-tenths of their constituents," Lyon infuriated the Federalists.

The situation simmered for two weeks, and on the morning of February 15, 1798, Federalist anger reached a boiling point when conservative Connecticut Congressman Roger Griswold attacked Lyon on the House floor with a hickory cane. As Congressman George Thatcher wrote in a letter now held at the Massachusetts Historical Society, "Mr. Griswald [sic] [was] laying on blows with all his might upon Mr. Lyon. Griswald continued his blows on the head, shoulder, & arms of Lyon, [who was] protecting his head & face as well as he could. Griswald tripped Lyon & threw him on the floor & gave him one or two [more] blows in the face."

A Senator Speaks Against an Earlier Patriot Act

On June 21, 1798, the last day of the congressional debates on the Alien and Sedition Acts, Senator Edward Livingston spoke the following words to the Senate:

> If we are ready to violate the Constitution, will the people submit to our unauthorized acts? Sir, they ought not to submit; they would deserve the chains that these measures are forging for them. The country will swarm with informers, spies, delators, and all the odious reptile tribe that breed in the sunshine of despotic power . . . The hours of the most unsuspected confidence, the intimacies of friendship, or the recesses of domestic retirement, afford no security. The companion whom you trust, the friend in whom you must confide, the domestic who waits in your chamber, are all tempted to betray your imprudent and unguarded follies; to misrepresent your words; to convey them, distorted by calumny, to the secret tribunal where jealousy presides—where fear officiates as accuser, and suspicion is the only evidence that is heard . . . Do not let us be told that we are to excite a fervor against a foreign aggression to establish a tyranny at home; that like the arch traitor we cry "Hail Columbia" at the moment we are betraying her to destruction; that we sing "Happy Land," when we are plunging it in ruin and disgrace; and that we are absurd enough to call ourselves free and enlightened while we advocate principles that would have disgraced the age of Gothic barbarity.

Jennifer Van Bergen, "Repeal the USA Patriot Act," April 6, 2002, truthout.com.

In sharp contrast to his predecessor George Washington, America's second president had succeeded in creating an atmosphere of fear and division in the new republic, and it brought out the worst in his conservative supporters. Across the new nation, Federalist mobs and Federalist-controlled police and militia attacked Democratic-Republican newspapers and shouted down or threatened individuals who dared speak out in public against John Adams.

Even members of Congress were not legally immune from the long arm of Adams' Alien and Sedition Acts. When Congressmen Lyon—already hated by the Federalists for his opposition to the law, and recently caned in Congress by Federalist Roger Griswold—wrote an article pointing out Adams' "continual grasp for power" and suggesting that Adams had an "unbounded thirst for ridiculous pomp, foolish adulation, and selfish avarice," Federalists convened a federal grand jury and indicted Congressman Lyon for bringing "the President and government of the United States into contempt."

Lyon, who had served in the Continental Army during the Revolutionary War, was led through the town of Vergennes, Vermont in shackles. He ran for re-election from his 12×16-foot Vergennes jail cell and handily won his seat. "It is quite a new kind of jargon," Lyon wrote from jail to his constituents, "to call a Representative of the People an Opposer of the Government because he does not, as a legislator, advocate and acquiesce in every proposition that comes from the Executive."

The Lessons of History

Which brings us to today. The possible ray of light for those who oppose the attempts of George W. Bush to emulate John Adams is found in the end of the story of Adams' attempt to suborn the Bill of Rights and turn the United States into a one-party state:

• The Alien and Sedition Acts caused the Democratic-Republican newspapers to become more popular than ever, and turned the inebriated Luther Baldwin into a national celebrity. In like fashion, progressive websites and talk shows are today proliferating across the internet, and victims of no-fly laws and illegal arrests at anti-Bush rallies are often featured on the web and on radio programs like *Democracy Now*.

- The day Adams signed the Acts, Thomas Jefferson left town in protest. Even though Jefferson was Vice President, and could theoretically benefit from using the Acts against his own political enemies, he and James Madison continued to protest and work against them. Jefferson wrote the text for a non-binding resolution against the Acts that was adopted by the Kentucky legislature, and James Madison wrote one for Virginia that was adopted by that legislature. Today, in similar fashion, over 100 communities across America have adopted resolutions against Bush's Patriot Act, and, in the spirit of Matthew Lyon, Vermont Congressman Bernie Sanders has introduced legislation to repeal parts of the Act.

- Jefferson beat Adams in the election of 1800 as a wave of voter revulsion over Adams' phony and self-serving "patriotism" swept over the nation (along with concerns about Adams' belligerent war rhetoric against the French). Today, even a minor appearance by Howard Dean or Dennis Kucinich—both on record for repealing much or all of the Patriot Act—draws a large crowd. There's a growing conviction across the nation that Dean—or possibly another non-DLC [Democratic Leadership Council] Democrat—can defeat Bush in 2004.

- When Jefferson exposed Adams as a poseur and tool of the powerful elite, the rot within Adams' Federalist Party was exposed along with it. The Federalists lost their hold on Congress in the election of 1800, and began a 30-year slide into total disintegration (later to be reincarnated as Whigs and then as Republicans). Today, as the Tom Delay and Roy Blount bribery scandals[2] widen, tax cuts for the rich are understood for what they are, and the corporate takeover of America is alarming average citizens, the rot in the Republican Party is more and more obvious. Americans are demanding representation for We, The People, and non-DLC Democrats, Greens, and Progressives can offer it.

2. House majority leader Tom Delay is accused of directing money from corporations and Washington lobbyists to Republican campaign coffers in Texas in 2001 and 2002 as part of a plan to redraw the state's congressional districts.

- In what came to be known as "The Revolution of 1800" or "The Second American Revolution," Thomas Jefferson freed all the men imprisoned by Adams as one of his first acts of office. Jefferson even reimbursed the fines they'd paid—with interest—and granted them a formal pardon and apology. Today, undoing the Patriot Act and kicking corporate money out of Washington D.C. have become popular progressive and Democratic campaign themes.

The history of John Adams' failed presidency gives hope and encouragement to those committed to real democracy and genuine freedom. History shows that when enough people become politically active, they can rescue the soul of America from sliding into a corrupt, abusive police state.

The future of our nation is now at risk just as much as it was in 1800: It's time to wake up and work to elect and empower politicians interested in real democracy. If we're successful, America may experience a revival every bit as extraordinary as that brought about by Jefferson's Second American Revolution.

Periodical Bibliography

The following articles have been selected to supplement the diverse views presented in this chapter.

Kerby Anderson — "Amend the Patriot Act?" *Probe Ministries International*, January 11, 2002. www.probe.org/docs/c-patriot.html.

James Jay Carafano and Paul Rosenzweig — "A Patriotic Day: 9/11 Commission Recognized Importance of the Patriot Act," *Web Memo*, April 15, 2004. www.heritage.org.

Cato Institute — "Security and Freedom in a Free Society," *Cato Policy Report*, September/October 2002.

Cato Institute — "USA Patriot Act and Domestic Detention Policy," *Cato Handbook for Congress*, 2004.

Rachel Coen — "Another Stealth Assault on Liberties? Muted Media Response to Ashcroft's Proposed Patriot Act II," *Extra!*, March/April 2003.

David Cole — "Patriot Act's Big Brother," *Nation*, March 17, 2004.

Timothy H. Edgar — "Watch Out America, the White House Is Seeking to Expand the Patriot Act," *Crisis*, November/December 2003.

Bob Egelko — "Congress Uses Scalpel to Cut Up Patriot Act," *San Francisco Chronicle*, September 10, 2003.

Samuel Francis — "New Patriot Act Ignores Real Source of Terrorism," *Conservative Chronicle*, April 30, 2003.

William F. Jasper — "Trading Freedom for Security," *New American*, May 5, 2003.

Charles Levendosky — "Congress Acts to Curb US Police Powers," *Progressive Populist*, September 1, 2003.

Charles Levendosky — "Victory Act No Victory for Public," *Liberal Opinion Week*, September 8, 2003.

Robert A. Levy — "The USA Patriot Act: We Deserve Better," *Cato Institute*, November 27, 2001.

Andrew P. Napolitano — "Repeal the Patriot Act," *Wall Street Journal*, March 10, 2004.

Jennifer Van Bergen — "Repeal the USA Patriot Act," *truthout*, April 1, 2002. www.truthout.org.

Tim Wheeler — "Nation Resounds to Call: Repeal the Patriot Act," *People's Weekly World*, December 6, 2003.

CHAPTER 4

How Have Americans Reacted to the Patriot Act?

Chapter Preface

"Be it resolved that the North Pole City Council requests members of the U.S. Congress to immediately re-examine the U.S.A. Patriot Act." A unanimous resolution passed by town leaders in North Pole, Alaska, a town of fifteen hundred people.

Although the Patriot Act passed with bipartisan support during a period of unprecedented national unity following the terrorist attacks of September 11, 2001, the following year opposition to the act spread across the nation. As of this writing, four states—Hawaii, Alaska, Maine, and Vermont—and 354 cities and counties have passed resolutions condemning the Patriot Act for violating civil liberties. Of these, some have gone even further, passing ordinances that bar community officials from cooperating with federal investigations using Patriot Act tools. What many commentators consider remarkable is the political and ideological diversity of the communities opposed to the act. American Civil Liberties Union (ACLU) counsel Timothy H. Edgar claims,

> Berkeley, California, that smoldering hotbed of liberalism, and the entire state of Alaska—known for its intrasigent support of the Republican Party—share nothing in common save one of these resolutions on their books. Resolutions have appeared in small towns in rock-ribbed conservative Idaho, where Republicans reign supreme, and in major cities like Chicago, long dominated by the Democratic Party.

The grassroots movement to oppose the Patriot Act began in Ann Arbor, Michigan. Residents of the city drafted a resolution in response to the arrest and detention of Arab-American and Muslim men who were suspected of being terrorists. The men were denied bond and open hearings. On January 20, 2002, city leaders passed a resolution rejecting racial profiling of any group in their community and called on the federal government to assure that all individuals be afforded due process. The signatories sent this resolution to their congressional delegation, U.S. attorney general John Ashcroft, and President George W. Bush. Arcata, a northern California city of approximately sixteen thousand people, was the first city to pass a law effectively nullifying the act in that city. The ordinance, passed in May 2003, imposes a fine of $57 on any city department head who voluntarily assists or cooperates with federal investigations in a way that violates civil liberties.

Some legal commentators question the validity of such resolutions and ordinances. Former presidential counsel John Dean supports the movement challenging the Patriot Act but warns that some resolutions are vulnerable to attack by the U.S. Justice Department. He illustrates his point using the example of the ACLU sample resolution that urges city councils to direct the city's police department to "refrain from participating in the enforcement of federal immigration laws." Dean claims that if local police do not comply with a deportation request from the Bureau of Immigration and Customs Enforcement, now part of the Department of Homeland Security, and that illegal alien turns out to be a terrorist, the Justice Department could bring obstruction of justice charges against the police and the city council members who draft such resolutions. Moreover, he contends, juries will likely be unsympathetic. "What jury will refuse to convict those who dragged their feet when a true terrorist needed to be deported from our shores?" Dean maintains. He suggests that such resolutions be drafted so that they do not pit state and local governments against the federal government. "The grassroots movement to respect the Bill of Rights even in the midst of the war on terrorism is too important to make mistakes," Dean concludes.

Patriot Act supporters contend that such resolutions and ordinances are a hysterical reaction to the act but differ in their concern over their impact. Political commentator Rich Lowry contends that proposals by Patriot Act critics protect terrorists. "If the ACLU gets its way on the Patriot Act," Lowry argues, "some future successful terrorists will want to remember it in their prayers." Other Patriot Act supporters remain unconcerned about the grassroots reaction, claiming it is part of the democratic process. Douglas Kmiec, dean of the law school at Catholic University of America, contends, "What you're seeing is an appropriate part of the American tradition—be it your county commission passing a resolution or the local librarian filing a suit. We work best this way."

"I will vote against [the Patriot Act] when the roll is called."

A U.S. Senator Opposes the Patriot Act

Russell Feingold

In the following viewpoint, excerpted from his statement delivered from the U.S. Senate floor on October 25, 2001, U.S. senator Russell Feingold explains why he will cast his vote against the Patriot Act. According to Feingold, the act fails to strike the right balance between protecting the American people from terrorism and preserving their freedom. He maintains that the act vastly expands police power to obtain information about Americans with little showing that the information is relevant to America's war on terrorism. Pressure to pass the act quickly without public debate threatens to erode the very liberties Congress is sworn to protect, he contends. Feingold was the only senator to vote against the Patriot Act.

As you read, consider the following questions:

1. What impact does the Patriot Act have on the Fourth Amendment, in Feingold's view?
2. How does the Patriot Act break down the distinction between intelligence and criminal investigations, in the author's opinion?
3. According to the author, what is troubling about allowing the federal government to detain and deport people engaged in innocent associational activity?

Russell Feingold, address to the U.S. Senate, Washington, DC, October 25, 2001.

I have asked for this time [on the Senate floor] to speak about the anti-terrorism bill before us, H.R. 3162 [the Patriot Act]. As we address this bill, we are especially mindful of the [September 11, 2001, terrorist attacks] and beyond, which led to the bill's proposal and its quick consideration in the Congress. . . .

Preserving our freedom is one of the main reasons that we are now engaged in this new war on terrorism. We will lose that war without firing a shot if we sacrifice the liberties of the American people.

A Need for Deliberation and Debate

That is why I found the anti-terrorism bill originally proposed by Attorney General [John] Ashcroft and President [George W.] Bush to be troubling.

The Administration's proposed bill contained vast new powers for law enforcement, some seemingly drafted in haste and others that came from the FBI's wish list that Congress has rejected in the past. You may remember that the Attorney General announced his intention to introduce a bill shortly after the September 11 attacks. He provided the text of the bill the following Wednesday, and urged Congress to enact it by the end of the week. That was plainly impossible, but the pressure to move on this bill quickly, without deliberation and debate, has been relentless ever since.

It is one thing to shortcut the legislative process in order to get federal financial aid to the cities hit by terrorism. We did that, and no one complained that we moved too quickly. It is quite another to press for the enactment of sweeping new powers for law enforcement that directly affect the civil liberties of the American people without due deliberation by the peoples' elected representatives.

Fortunately, cooler heads prevailed at least to some extent, and while this bill has been on a fast track, there has been time to make some changes and reach agreement on a bill that is less objectionable than the bill that the Administration originally proposed. . . .

My focus on this bill, as Chair of the Constitution Subcommittee of the Judiciary Committee in the Senate, was on those provisions that implicate our constitutional freedoms.

And it was in reviewing those provisions that I came to feel that the Administration's demand for haste was inappropriate; indeed, it was dangerous. Our process in the Senate, as truncated as it was, did lead to the elimination or significant rewriting of a number of audacious proposals that I and many other members found objectionable. . . .

So the bill before us is certainly improved from the bill that the Administration sent to us on September 19, [2001] and wanted us to pass on September 21. But again, in my judgement, it does not strike the right balance between empowering law enforcement and protecting constitutional freedoms. Let me take a moment to discuss some of the shortcomings of the bill.

Changing Criminal Procedure

First, the bill contains some very significant changes in criminal procedure that will apply to every federal criminal investigation in this country, not just those involving terrorism. One provision would greatly expand the circumstances in which law enforcement agencies can search homes and offices without notifying the owner prior to the search. The long-standing practice under the Fourth Amendment of serving a warrant prior to executing a search could be easily avoided in virtually every case, because the government would simply have to show that it has "reasonable cause to believe" that providing notice "may" "seriously jeopardize an investigation." This is a significant infringement on personal liberty.

Notice is a key element of Fourth Amendment protections. It allows a person to point out mistakes in a warrant and to make sure that a search is limited to the terms of a warrant. Just think about the possibility of the police showing up at your door with a warrant to search your house. You look at the warrant and say, "yes, that's my address, but the name on the warrant isn't me." And the police realize a mistake has been made and go away. If you're not home, and the police have received permission to do a "sneak and peak" search, they can come in your house, look around, and leave, and may never have to tell you.

Another very troubling provision has to do with the effort

to combat computer crime. The bill allows law enforcement to monitor a computer with the permission of its owner or operator, without the need to get a warrant or show probable cause. That's fine in the case of a so called "denial of service attack" or plain old computer hacking. A computer owner should be able to give the police permission to monitor communications coming from what amounts to a trespasser on the computer.

As drafted in the Senate bill, however, the provision might permit an employer to give permission to the police to monitor the e-mails of an employee who has used her computer at work to shop for Christmas gifts. Or someone who uses a computer at a library or at school and happens to go to a gambling or pornography site in violation of the Internet use policies of the library or the university might also be subjected to government surveillance—without probable cause and without any time limit. With this one provision, Fourth Amendment protections are potentially eliminated for a broad spectrum of electronic communications.

Expanding Government Power

I am also very troubled by the broad expansion of government power under the Foreign Intelligence Surveillance Act, known as FISA. When Congress passed FISA in 1978 it granted to the executive branch the power to conduct surveillance in foreign intelligence investigations without meeting the rigorous probable cause standard under the Fourth Amendment that is required for criminal investigations. There is a lower threshold for obtaining a wiretap order from the FISA court because the FBI is not investigating a crime, it is investigating foreign intelligence activities. But the law currently requires that intelligence gathering be the primary purpose of the investigation in order for this lower standard to apply.

This bill changes that requirement. The government now will only have to show that intelligence is a "significant purpose" of the investigation. So even if the *primary* purpose is a criminal investigation, the heightened protections of the Fourth Amendment won't apply.

It seems obvious that with this lower standard, the FBI

will try to use FISA as much as it can. And of course, with terrorism investigations that won't be difficult, because the terrorists are apparently sponsored or at least supported by foreign governments. This means that the Fourth Amendment rights will be significantly curtailed in many investigations of terrorist acts.

The significance of the breakdown of the distinction between intelligence and criminal investigations becomes apparent when you see the other expansions of government power under FISA in this bill. One provision that troubles me a great deal is a provision that permits the government under FISA to compel the production of records from any business regarding any person, if that information is sought in connection with an investigation of terrorism or espionage.

Now we're not talking here about travel records pertaining to a terrorist suspect, which we all can see can be highly relevant to an investigation of a terrorist plot. FISA already gives the FBI the power to get airline, train, hotel, car rental and other records of a suspect.

Conducting Fishing Expeditions

But under this bill, the government can compel the disclosure of the personal records of anyone—perhaps someone who worked with, or lived next door to, or went to school with, or sat on an airplane with, or has been seen in the company of, or whose phone number was called by—the target of the investigation.

And under this new provision *all* business records can be compelled, including those containing sensitive personal information like medical records from hospitals or doctors, or educational records, or records of what books someone has taken out of the library. This is an enormous expansion of authority, under a law that provides only minimal judicial supervision.

Under this provision, the government can apparently go on a fishing expedition and collect information on virtually anyone. All it has to allege in order to get an order for these records from the court is that the information is sought for an investigation of international terrorism or clandestine intelligence gathering. That's it. On that minimal showing in an ex parte application to a secret court, with no showing even that the information is *relevant* to the investigation, the government can lawfully compel a doctor or hospital to release medical records, or a library to release circulation records. This is a truly breathtaking expansion of police power.

Questioning the Immigration Provisions

Let me turn to a final area of real concern about this legislation, which I think brings us full circle to the cautions I expressed on the day after the attacks. There are two very troubling provisions dealing with our immigration laws in this bill.

Keefe. © 2002 by Cagle Cartoons, Inc. Reproduced by permission.

First, the Administration's original proposal would have granted the Attorney General extraordinary powers to detain immigrants indefinitely, including legal permanent residents. The Attorney General could do so based on mere suspicion that the person is engaged in terrorism. I believe the Administration was really over-reaching here, and I am pleased that Senator [Patrick] Leahy was able to negotiate some protections. The Senate bill now requires the Attorney General to charge the immigrant within seven days with a criminal offense or immigration violation. In the event that the Attorney General does not charge the immigrant, the immigrant must be released.

While this protection is an improvement, the provision remains fundamentally flawed. Even with this seven-day charging requirement, the bill would nevertheless continue to permit the indefinite detention in two situations. First, immigrants who win their deportation cases could continue to be held if the Attorney General continues to have suspicions.

Second, this provision creates a deep unfairness to immigrants who are found not to be deportable for terrorism but have an immigration status violation, such as overstaying a visa. If the immigration judge finds that they are eligible for relief from deportation, and therefore can stay in the country because, for example, they have long-standing family ties here, the Attorney General could continue to hold them.

Now, I am pleased that the final version of the legislation includes a few improvements over the bill that passed the Senate. In particular, the bill would require the Attorney General to review the detention decision every six months and would allow only the Attorney General or Deputy Attorney General, not lower level officials, to make that determination. While I am pleased these provisions are included in the bill, I believe it still falls short of meeting even basic constitutional standards of due process and fairness. The bill continues to allow the Attorney General to detain persons based on mere suspicion. Our system normally requires higher standards of proof for a deprivation of liberty. For example, deportation proceedings are subject to a clear and convincing evidence standard. Criminal convictions, of course, require proof beyond a reasonable doubt.

The bill also continues to deny detained persons a trial or hearing where the government would be required to prove that the person is, in fact, engaged in terrorist activity. This is unjust and inconsistent with the values our system of justice holds dearly.

Guilt by Association

Another provision in the bill that deeply troubles me allows the detention and deportation of people engaging in innocent associational activity. It would allow for the detention and deportation of individuals who provide lawful assistance to groups that are not even designated by the Secretary of State as terrorist organizations, but instead have engaged in vaguely defined "terrorist activity" sometime in the past. To avoid deportation, the immigrant is required to prove a negative: that he or she did not know, and should not have known, that the assistance would further terrorist activity.

This language creates a very real risk that truly innocent individuals could be deported for innocent associations with humanitarian or political groups that the government later chooses to regard as terrorist organizations. Groups that might fit this definition could include Operation Rescue [an anti-abortion organization], Greenpeace [an environmental organization], and even the Northern Alliance [an Afghanistani rebel movement] fighting the Taliban [an Islamic fundamentalist government ruling Afghanistan] in northern Afghanistan. This provision amounts to "guilt by association," which I believe violates the First Amendment.

And speaking of the First Amendment, under this bill, a lawful permanent resident who makes a controversial speech that the government deems to be supportive of terrorism might be barred from returning to his or her family after taking a trip abroad.

Despite assurances from the Administration at various points in this process that these provisions that implicate associational activity would be improved, there have been no changes in the bill on these points since it passed the Senate.

Now here's where my cautions in the aftermath of the terrorist attacks and my concern over the reach of the anti-terrorism bill come together. To the extent that the expansive new immigration powers that the bill grants to the Attorney General are subject to abuse, who do we think is most likely to bear the brunt of that abuse? It won't be immigrants from Ireland, it won't be immigrants from El Salvador or Nicaragua, it won't even be immigrants from Haiti or Africa. It will be immigrants from Arab, Muslim, and South Asian countries. In the wake of these terrible events, our government has been given vast new powers and they may fall most heavily on a minority of our population who already feel particularly acutely the pain of this disaster.

When concerns of this kind have been raised with the Administration and supporters of this bill they have told us, "don't worry, the FBI would never do that." I call on the Attorney General and the Justice Department to ensure that my fears are not borne out.

The anti-terrorism bill that we consider in the Senate today highlights the march of technology, and how that march cuts both for and against personal liberty. Justice Brandeis foresaw some of the future in a 1928 dissent, when he wrote:

> The progress of science in furnishing the Government with means of espionage is not likely to stop with wire-tapping. Ways may some day be developed by which the Government, without removing papers from secret drawers, can reproduce them in court, and by which it will be enabled to expose to a jury the most intimate occurrences of the home. . . . Can it be that the Constitution affords no protection against such invasions of individual security?

We must grant law enforcement the tools that it needs to stop this terrible threat. But we must give them only those extraordinary tools that they need and that relate specifically to the task at hand.

Trading Liberty for Security

In the play, "A Man for All Seasons," Sir Thomas More questions the bounder Roper whether he would level the forest of English laws to punish the Devil. "What would you do?" More asks, "Cut a great road through the law to get after the Devil?" Roper affirms, "I'd cut down every law in England to do that." To which More replies:

> And when the last law was down, and the Devil turned round on you—where would you hide, Roper, the laws all being flat? This country's planted thick with laws from coast to coast . . . and if you cut them down . . . d'you really think you could stand upright in the winds that would blow then? Yes, I'd give the Devil benefit of law, for my own safety's sake.

We must maintain our vigilance to preserve our laws and our basic rights.

We in this body have a duty to analyze, to test, to weigh new laws that the zealous and often sincere advocates of security would suggest to us. This is what I have tried to do with this anti-terrorism bill. And that is why I will vote against this bill when the roll is called.

Protecting the safety of the American people is a solemn duty of the Congress; we must work tirelessly to prevent more tragedies like the devastating attacks of September 11th. We must prevent more children from losing their mothers, more wives from losing their husbands, and more firefighters from losing their heroic colleagues. But the Congress will fulfill its duty only when it protects *both* the American people and the freedoms at the foundation of American society. So let us preserve our heritage of basic rights. Let us practice as well as preach that liberty. And let us fight to maintain that freedom that we call America.

> *"With my signature, [the Patriot Act] will give intelligence and law enforcement officials important new tools to fight a present danger."*

The President of the United States Signs the Patriot Act into Law

George W. Bush

The Patriot Act gives intelligence and law enforcement the tools they need to pursue and punish terrorists and prevent future terrorist attacks, argues President George W. Bush in the following viewpoint, originally given as remarks at the signing of the Patriot Act into law on October 26, 2001. The act allows law enforcement and intelligence agencies to share information, he asserts. Moreover, Bush maintains, the act provides law enforcement with up-to-date tools to fight modern terrorists. By an overwhelming majority, Congress passed the Patriot Act, a well-crafted document that protects civil liberties, he contends.

As you read, consider the following questions:
1. According to Bush, what is the purpose of the Patriot Act?
2. In the author's opinion, how were investigations slowed by the limit on the reach of federal search warrants?
3. How does the Patriot Act change statutes that dealt more severely with drug-traffickers than with terrorists, in the author's view?

George W. Bush, address to the nation, Washington, DC, October 26, 2001.

Today [October 26, 2001], we take an essential step in defeating terrorism, while protecting the constitutional rights of all Americans. With my signature, this law [the USA Patriot Act] will give intelligence and law enforcement officials important new tools to fight a present danger.

I commend the House and Senate for the hard work they put into this legislation. Members of Congress and their staffs spent long nights and weekends to get this important bill to my desk. I appreciate their efforts, and bipartisanship, in passing this new law. . . .

Countering Terrorism

The changes, effective today, will help counter a threat like no other our nation has ever faced. We've seen the enemy, and the murder of thousands of innocent, unsuspecting people [during the September 11, 2001, terrorist attacks]. They recognize no barrier of morality. They have no conscience. The terrorists cannot be reasoned with. . . .

One thing is for certain: These terrorists must be pursued, they must be defeated, and they must be brought to justice. And that is the purpose of this legislation. Since the 11th of September, the men and women of our intelligence and law enforcement agencies have been relentless in their response to new and sudden challenges.

We have seen the horrors terrorists can inflict. We may never know what horrors our country was spared by the diligent and determined work of our police forces, the FBI, ATF [Bureau of Alcohol, Tobacco, Firearms and Explosives] agents, federal marshals, Custom officers, Secret Service, intelligence professionals and local law enforcement officials, under the most trying conditions. They are serving this country with excellence, and often with bravery.

Providing Better Tools

They deserve our full support and every means of help that we can provide. We're dealing with terrorists who operate by highly sophisticated methods and technologies, some of which were not even available when our existing laws were written. The bill before me takes account of the new realities and dangers posed by modern terrorists. It will help law enforcement to identify, to dismantle, to disrupt, and to punish terrorists before they strike.

For example, this legislation gives law enforcement officials better tools to put an end to financial counterfeiting, smuggling and money-laundering. Secondly, it gives intelligence operations and criminal operations the chance to operate not on separate tracks, but to share vital information so necessary to disrupt a terrorist attack before it occurs.

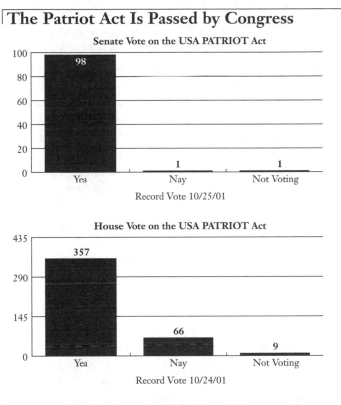

The Patriot Act Is Passed by Congress

Senate Vote on the USA PATRIOT Act

Record Vote 10/25/01

House Vote on the USA PATRIOT Act

Record Vote 10/24/01

Department of Justice, *Preserving Life & Liberty*, 2004.

As of today, we're changing the laws governing information-sharing. And as importantly, we're changing the culture of our various agencies that fight terrorism. Countering and investigating terrorist activity is the number one priority for both law enforcement and intelligence agencies.

Surveillance of communications is another essential tool

to pursue and stop terrorists. The existing law was written in the era of rotary telephones. This new law that I sign today will allow surveillance of all communications used by terrorists, including e-mails, the Internet, and cell phones.

Expanding Federal Reach

As of today, we'll be able to better meet the technological challenges posed by this proliferation of communications technology. Investigations are often slowed by limit on the reach of federal search warrants.

Law enforcement agencies have to get a new warrant for each new district they investigate, even when they're after the same suspect. Under this new law, warrants are valid across all districts and across all states. And, finally, the new legislation greatly enhances the penalties that will fall on terrorists or anyone who helps them.

Current statutes deal more severely with drug-traffickers than with terrorists. That changes today. We are enacting new and harsh penalties for possession of biological weapons. We're making it easier to seize the assets of groups and individuals involved in terrorism. The government will have wider latitude in deporting known terrorists and their supporters. The statute of limitations on terrorist acts will be lengthened, as will prison sentences for terrorists.

This bill was carefully drafted and considered. Led by the members of Congress on this stage, and those seated in the audience, it was crafted with skill and care, determination and a spirit of bipartisanship for which the entire nation is grateful. This bill met with an overwhelming—overwhelming agreement in Congress, because it upholds and respects the civil liberties guaranteed by our Constitution.

This legislation is essential not only to pursuing and punishing terrorists, but also preventing more atrocities in the hands of the evil ones. This government will enforce this law with all the urgency of a nation at war. The elected branches of our government, and both political parties, are united in our resolve to fight and stop and punish those who would do harm to the American people.

It is now my honor to sign into law the USA Patriot Act of 2001.

"The American Library Association urges librarians everywhere to defend and support user privacy."

Librarians Protest the Patriot Act

American Library Association

The Patriot Act permits the federal government to examine the library records of patrons without their knowledge. In the following viewpoint the American Library Association (ALA) argues that the Patriot Act violates library user pri vacy and thus constitutes a threat to free access to knowledge and information. The freedom to seek knowledge and express ideas is a fundamental right that should be protected in a democratic society, the ALA maintains. The association urges librarians to oppose the use of government power to suppress the open exchange of information. An association of over sixty-four thousand members, the ALA promotes quality library and information services and public access to information.

As you read, consider the following questions:

1. In a library, what should not be examined or scrutinized by others, according to the ALA?
2. What activities of library users may be under government surveillance without their knowledge or consent, in the author's opinion?
3. In the author's opinion, what policies should all libraries adopt and implement?

American Library Association, "Resolution of the USA Patriot Act and Related Measures That Infringe on the Rights of Library Users," www.ala.org, January 29, 2003. Copyright © 2003 by the American Library Association. Reproduced by permission.

The American Library Association affirms the responsibility of the leaders of the United States to protect and preserve the freedoms that are the foundation of our democracy. . . . Libraries are a critical force for promoting the free flow and unimpeded distribution of knowledge and information for individuals, institutions, and communities. . . . The American Library Association holds that suppression of ideas undermines a democratic society and . . . privacy is essential to the exercise of free speech, free thought, and free association. . . . In a library, the subject of users' interests should not be examined or scrutinized by others. . . .

Threatening Liberties

Certain provisions of the USA PATRIOT Act, the revised Attorney General Guidelines to the Federal Bureau of Investigation, and other related measures expand the authority of the federal government to investigate citizens and noncitizens, to engage in surveillance, and to threaten civil rights and liberties guaranteed under the United States Constitution and Bill of Rights. . . . The USA PATRIOT Act and other recently enacted laws, regulations, and guidelines increase the likelihood that the activities of library users, including their use of computers to browse the Web or access e-mail, may be under government surveillance without their knowledge or consent.

Now, therefore, be it resolved that the American Library Association opposes any use of governmental power to suppress the free and open exchange of knowledge and information or to intimidate individuals exercising free inquiry. . . . The American Library Association encourages all librarians, library administrators, library governing bodies, and library advocates to educate their users, staff, and communities about the process for compliance with the USA PATRIOT Act and other related measures and about the dangers to individual privacy and the confidentiality of library records resulting from those measures. . . .

Defending User Privacy

Be it further resolved that the American Library Association urges librarians everywhere to defend and support user privacy and free and open access to knowledge and information. . . . The American Library Association will work with other organizations, as appropriate, to protect the rights of inquiry and free expression. . . . The American Library Association will take actions as appropriate to obtain and publicize information about the surveillance of libraries and library users by law enforcement agencies and to assess the impact on library users and their communities. . . . The American Library Association urges all libraries to adopt and implement patron privacy and record retention policies that affirm that "the collection of personally identifiable information should only be a matter of routine or policy when necessary for the fulfillment of the mission of the library.". . .

The American Library Association considers sections of the USA PATRIOT Act are a present danger to the constitutional rights and privacy rights of library users and urges the United States Congress to:

1. provide active oversight of the implementation of the USA PATRIOT Act and other related measures, and the revised Attorney General Guidelines to the Federal Bureau of Investigation;

2. hold hearings to determine the extent of the surveillance on library users and their communities; and

3. amend or change the sections of these laws and the guidelines that threaten or abridge the rights of inquiry and free expression. . . .

This resolution [should] be forwarded to the President of the United States, to the Attorney General of the United States, to Members of both Houses of Congress, to the library community, and to others as appropriate.

"The Patriot Act has been our laser-guided weapon to prevent terrorist attacks."

The U.S. Attorney General Reports on the Patriot Act's Successes

John Ashcroft

The Patriot Act has been a successful weapon in America's war on terrorism, claims John Ashcroft in the following viewpoint, originally given as remarks made upon release of the Department of Justice *Report from the Field: The USA PA-TRIOT Act at Work* on July 15, 2004. This report, Ashcroft maintains, is evidence that the Patriot Act saves lives by giving federal law enforcement the tools it needs to protect Americans from terrorists and violent criminals. To take away these tools would be to disarm those who are trying to protect American citizens, Ashcroft asserts. Ashcroft was U.S. attorney general when the Patriot Act was proposed, passed, and implemented.

As you read, consider the following questions:
1. According to Ashcroft, how has the government used tools in the Patriot Act to combat serious crime?
2. What has been the effect of removing "The Wall" between law enforcement and the intelligence community, in the author's opinion?
3. In the author's view, what does the Department of Justice report help reinforce?

John Ashcroft, address to the U.S. Congress, Washington, DC, July 13, 2004.

195

In Afghanistan, our Special Operations Forces have deployed state-of-the-art weaponry and cutting edge tactics to hunt [the terrorist group] al Qaeda and destroy their safe haven.

Here at home, our domestic warriors—federal, state and local law enforcement—have used the new legal tools and technology in the Patriot Act to hunt down al Qaeda, destroy their safe haven, and save American lives.

Let me be clear about something before I move on: Congress intended that the Patriot Act be used to save lives from terrorist attacks. In fact, there are a number of provisions that are only to be used to prevent terrorism or foreign spying.

But other tools in the Patriot Act were developed to combat serious crime across the board, and we have used those general tools both in terrorism cases as well as in other cases, such as to catch predatory child molesters and pornographers.

We are a nation at war. That is a fact. Al Qaeda wants to hit us and hit us hard. We have to use every legal weapon available to protect the American people from terrorist attacks.

Like the smart bombs, laser-guided missiles and predator drones employed by our armed forces to hunt and kill al Qaeda in Afghanistan, the Patriot Act is just as vital to targeting the terrorists who would kill our people and destroy our freedom here at home.

The Patriot Act's Success

I am pleased . . . to have met with . . . distinguished members of Congress and to have presented to them a report on how the Patriot Act has been our laser-guided weapon to prevent terrorist attacks. I have also been pleased to discuss how we have used the Patriot Act to save lives from violent criminals who prey on the vulnerable.

This report is an unprecedented compilation of dozens of real life cases from across the country in which the FBI and other law enforcement officials have used the tools of the Patriot Act to protect America's families and communities, and even to save lives.

In fact, this report provides a mountain of evidence that the Patriot Act has saved lives.

By tearing down the wall between law enforcement and

the intelligence community, we have been able to share information in a way that was virtually impossible before the Patriot Act.

The removal of "The Wall" and the dramatic increase in information sharing allowed by the Patriot Act has enabled us to hunt down and dismantle terror cells in Portland, Oregon; Lackawanna, New York; and Northern Virginia.

The information-sharing and coordination made possible by section 218 assisted the prosecution in San Diego of several persons involved in an al Qaeda drugs-for-weapons plot, which culminated in several guilty pleas. They admitted that they conspired to receive, as partial payment for heroin and hashish, four "Stinger" anti-aircraft missiles that they then intended to sell to the Taliban, an organization they knew at the time to be affiliated with al Qaeda.

The Effect of Taking Away Needed Tools

To allow section 218 and the other provisions of the Act to sunset at the end of next year [2005] would be paramount to unilateral disarmament against al Qaeda.

To take away the smart bombs, advanced night-vision equipment, and 21st Century communications capabilities from our soldiers, sailors, airmen and Marines would gut their ability to hunt and destroy al Qaeda terrorists.

To let the Patriot Act's laser-guided tools sunset would be to disarm the FBI and rollback our ability to target terrorism here at home, and would return us to the vulnerabilities we faced before September 11, 2001.

The Patriot Act is al Qaeda's worst nightmare when it comes to disrupting and disabling their operations here in America. Our law enforcement and intelligence teams have never before been so integrated and coordinated, and technologically-equipped, to target the 21st Century threat of global terror.

Using the Act Against Violent Criminals

The Patriot Act has also allowed us to go after violent criminals who would harm the innocent.

In Kentucky, law enforcement used section 210 of the Patriot Act to investigate an individual linked to several sexual assaults of children at public libraries and local parks. Just before the individual in question became the primary suspect in the case, he attempted to rape and abduct a six-year-old girl at a playground in Boone County, Kentucky.

The Tools of the Patriot Act

[The Department of Justice does] believe that subpoenas issued by grand juries comprised of United States citizens, and search warrants issued by a judge upon a showing of probable cause, allow us to make progress in the war on terror. The use of subpoenas and warrants has long been a standard investigative technique in virtually every type of criminal investigation. Justice Department prosecutors have done no more than make use of these centuries-old legal tools to fight a 21st-century war.

In order to effectively fight terrorism, we must gather information about the terrorists' plots. In the aftermath of [the terrorist attacks of September 11, 2001] thousands of subpoenas and court orders were issued so we could learn about the 19 hijackers' travels, the places they lived or stayed, their associates, the people they encountered, the phones, banks, or rental stores they used. Without the use of grand-jury subpoenas and judicially approved search warrants, we would not have the wealth of information that we have about the 19 hijackers and their associates today.

Barbara Comstock, *National Review*, September 3, 2003.

Investigators used section 210 to obtain key information from an Internet service provider. Within 20 minutes of receipt of the subpoena, the investigators obtained the information that allowed them to get a search warrant of the suspect's residence. Without that information, it is unlikely that investigators could have obtained a search warrant for the house.

Evidence located in the house proved essential in the arrest of the suspect and his wife within 24 hours. The couple was charged and prosecuted for 100-counts of receipt and possession of child pornography.

The prosecution also led to information tying the couple to multiple sexual assaults in Kentucky and Virginia. The defendants were convicted and sentenced to prison terms of approximately 30 years and 90 years.

In another example, Section 212 was instrumental in quickly rescuing a 13-year-old girl from Western Pennsylvania who had been lured from her home and was being held captive in Virginia by a 38-year-old man she had met online.

An anonymous caller contacted the FBI and stated that he had chatted online recently with an individual claiming to have taken a girl from Pittsburgh.

Based on information provided by that caller, FBI agents in Pittsburgh quickly requested information from an Internet service provider pursuant to section 212.

With the information provided in response to that request, agents were able to locate the kidnapper. They immediately went to his residence in Herndon, Virginia, and rescued the child victim. The suspect subsequently was arrested, pleaded guilty to charges of travel with intent to engage in sexual activity with a minor and sexual exploitation of a minor, and was sentenced to over 19 years in prison.

There are those who have criticized us for using the Patriot Act aggressively both in our war with al Qaeda and to protect the innocent from criminal predators.

This report will help reinforce what the majority of Americans already know: When it comes to saving lives and protecting freedom, we must use the Patriot Act and every legal means available to us.

*"[The National League of Cities] strongly
urges the U.S. Congress . . . to restore and
protect our nation's fundamental and
inalienable rights and liberties."*

U.S. Cities Oppose Sections of the Patriot Act

National League of Cities

In the following viewpoint the National League of Cities (NLC), the oldest and largest national organization for American cities, argues that the federal government must protect its citizens from terrorist attacks but not at the expense of fundamental civil liberties. The NLC claims that several sections of the Patriot Act allow the federal government to obtain the personal records of American citizens based on limited evidence and without notice. The NLC also asserts that compliance with the act's provision is putting a financial strain on U.S. cities.

As you read, consider the following questions:
1. What is required to protect American citizens against future terrorist attacks, in the NLC's view?
2. In the author's opinion, what does the legislation known as Patriot II contain?
3. What legislative action does the NLC support?

National League of Cities, "Resolution #2004-37: Resolution Affirming the Principles of Federalism and Civil Liberties," December 2003.

The National League of Cities (NLC) believes there is no inherent conflict between national security and the preservation of liberty, and affirms its strong support of the rights of Americans to be both safe and free. . . . NLC recognizes the Constitution of the United States as our nation's charter of liberty, and that the Bill of Rights enshrines the fundamental and inalienable rights of America, including the freedoms of speech, religion, assembly, privacy. . . . NLC has a distinguished record of upholding the Constitution, and the Bill of Rights, and safeguarding the freedoms and rights of American residents. . . .

Responding to Terrorism

On September 11, 2001, terrorists from abroad attacked the U.S. by commandeering four commercial airliners, and destroyed the World Trade Center in New York, significantly damaged the Pentagon, and caused a jetliner crash resulting in significant civilian casualties. . . . The terrorist attack was an attack on a nation that is home to a diverse population and plunged the nation into deep concern regarding its national security and vulnerability to future attacks. . . . NLC condemns all terrorist acts wherever occurring . . . and . . . believes that efforts to prevent and respond to acts of terrorism require extensive coordination, cooperation, and accountability among the federal, state, and local level. . . . NLC recognizes that protecting our citizens against future terrorist attacks requires the federal government to aggressively pursue potential terrorists but these efforts to combat terrorism should not disproportionately infringe on the essential civil rights and liberties of the people of the U.S. . . . The prevention of future terrorist attacks is a critical national priority, but it is equally important to preserve the fundamental civil liberties and personal freedoms embodied in the Bill of Rights over 200 years ago, and which have been preserved through a constant vigilance against periodic threats to its principles. . . .

A Dangerous Response

In response to the terrorist attacks, on October 26, 2001, the U.S. Congress passed, and President [George W.] Bush

The Right to Resist

Faced with what appeared to be overwhelming odds, a handful of people resisted the British Empire and planted the seeds of democracy—all rooted in the right to resist illegitimate government actions. As one of those fearless patriots, Thomas Jefferson, proclaimed: "The spirit of resistance to government is so valuable on certain occasions that I wish it to be always kept alive." Now, in a fitting tribute to the man who crafted our Declaration of Independence, Jefferson's hometown of Charlottesville, Va., has added its name to the growing list of cities opposing the U.S.A. Patriot Act.

John W. Whitehead, Rutherford Institute, July 28, 2003. www.rutherford.org.

signed into law, the USA PATRIOT Act, an acronym for "Uniting and Strengthening America by Providing Appropriate Tools Required to Intercept and Obstruct Terrorism," by a Senate vote of 98-1 and House of Representative vote of 357-66. . . . NLC believes that a number of provisions of the USA PATRIOT Act threaten fundamental rights and civil liberties, including:

- Section 213 which permits law enforcement to perform searches with no one present and to delay notification of the search of a citizen's home;
- Section 215 which permits the FBI Director to seek records from bookstores and libraries including books of patrons based on minimal evidence of wrongdoing and prohibits librarians and bookstore employees from disclosing the fact that they have been ordered to produce such documents;
- Section 218 which amends the "probable cause" requirement before conducting secret searches or surveillance to obtain evidence of a crime;
- Sections 215, 218, 358, and 508 which permit law enforcement authorities to have broad access to sensitive mental health, library, business, financial, and educational records despite the existence of previously adopted state and federal laws which were intended to strengthen the protection of these types of records;
- Sections 411 and 412 which give the Secretary of State broad powers to designate domestic groups as "terrorist organizations" and the Attorney General power to sub-

ject immigrants to indefinite detention or deportation even if no crime has been committed; and

- Sections 507 and 508 which impose an unfunded mandate on state and local public universities who must collect information on students that may be of interest to the Attorney General.

Municipal government budgets across the nation are strained and these added duties constitute unfunded mandates on cities' police departments, libraries, universities, etc. that cities cannot financially absorb. . . .

New legislation has been drafted entitled the Domestic Security Enhancement Act (DSEA) (also known as PATRIOT II)[1] which contains numerous new sweeping law enforcement and intelligence gathering powers, many of which are not related to terrorism, and which would severely dilute, if not undermine, many basic constitutional rights. . . . In response to the threats against civil liberties embodied in certain provisions of the PATRIOT Act, legislation has been introduced in the House and Senate that would roll back certain provisions of the PATRIOT Act.[2]

A Commitment to the Constitution

Now, therefore, be it resolved that NLC supports the U.S. campaign against terrorism, but NLC affirms its commitment to the U.S. Constitution and respective state constitutions. . . . NLC urges the President, and executive branch members to review, revise and rescind executive orders and policies adopted since the terrorist attacks, that limit or compromise the liberties guaranteed by the Constitution and the Bill of Rights. . . . NLC strongly urges the U.S. Congress to amend the PATRIOT Act in order to restore and protect our nation's fundamental and inalienable rights

1. PATRIOT II has not been officially introduced in either house of Congress and has no official standing. Some claim, however, that portions of the drafted bill have been attached to other bills.   2. Numerous bills have been proposed in both the House and the Senate to roll back provisions of the PATRIOT Act. Some have failed, such as Vermont representative Bernie Sanders' Freedom to Read Protection Act of 2003, an effort to repeal a controversial provision of the USA PATRIOT Act that allows the FBI to monitor people's reading, e-mail, and Internet habits at public libraries. Others, such as the Security and Freedom Ensured (SAFE) Act of 2003, which would roll back provisions of the Patriot Act such as the use of "sneak and peek" search warrants, remain in committee as of September 2004.

and liberties. . . . NLC supports the "Freedom to Read Protection Act of 2003" that would reinstate legal standards for libraries and bookstores and the Protecting the Rights of Individuals Act which would require a court order before conducting electronic surveillance. . . . NLC supports the sunset of key provisions of the PATRIOT Act and increased Congressional oversight over the role of the agencies responsible for enforcing the law. . . . NLC calls on Congress, the Department of Homeland Security, and other related agencies to partner with cities to protect our hometowns while simultaneously preserving the liberties of Americans.

Periodical Bibliography

The following articles have been selected to supplement the diverse views presented in this chapter.

Steve Brown	"PATRIOT Act Opponents Draw Justice Department's Ire," *CNSNews.com*, October 16, 2003.
Scott Carlson and Andrea L. Foster	"Colleges Fear Anti-Terrorism Law Could Turn Them into Big Brother," *Chronicle of Higher Education*, March 1, 2002.
Holly Edwards	"Grass-Roots Fight Against Patriot Act Makes Odd Politics," *Tennessean*, September 22, 2003.
Electronic Privacy Information Center	"The USA PATRIOT Act," *Electronic Privacy Information Center*, July 29, 2004. www.epic.org.
Free Expression Network	"The USA PATRIOT Act Six Months Later: A Statement by Members of the Free Expression Network," *Free Expression Network*, April 26, 2002.
Nat Hentoff	"Grassroots Patriots," *Progressive*, July 2002.
Issues & Controversies	"USA Patriot Act," December 13, 2002.
Nancy Kranich	"The Impact of the USA PATRIOT Act: An Update," *Free Expression Policy Project*, August 27, 2003. www.fepproject.org.
Charles Levendosky	"Patriot Act Faces Grasroots Defiance," *Liberal Opinion*, January 6, 2003.
Dahlia Lithwick and Julia Turner	"A Guide to the Patriot Act," *Slate*, September 8, 2003. www.slate.msn.com.
Rich Lowry	"Patriot Hysteria," *National Review Online*, August 28, 2003. www.nationalreview.com.
Eric A. Posner and John Yoo	"Panic and the Patriot Act," *Wall Street Journal*, December 9, 2003.
Nicole Rivard	"USA Patriot Act: How to Be Response Ready," *University Business*, May 2002.
Dean Schabner	"Patriot Revolution? Cities from Cambridge to Berkeley Reject Anti-Terror Measure," *ABC News.com*, July 1, 2002.
John W. Whitehead	"American Cities Show Spirit of Resistance to U.S.A. Patriot Act," *Rutherford Institute*, July 28, 2003.
John W. Whitehead	"Life, Liberty and the Pursuit of Terrorists: A Rutherford Institute Response to Attorney General John Ashcroft's 'Patriot Act Tour' and Website," *Rutherford Institute*, August 27, 2003.

For Further Discussion

Chapter 1

1. John Yoo and Eric Posner contend that the rhetoric used by both Patriot Act supporters and detractors does not focus on whether the act is actually the best strategy to enhance national security. Instead, they contend, supporters want to prove that the government is confronting the terrorist threat while critics want to assert the value of civil liberties. What evidence do you find within the other viewpoints in this chapter to support Yoo and Posner's claim? Explain, citing from the viewpoints.

2. John Ashcroft contends that the Patriot Act provides the federal government with new tools necessary to fight terrorism. Peter Erlinder claims that federal law enforcement had the tools needed to prevent terrorism before the Patriot Act. Citing from the viewpoints, explain which argument you find more persuasive.

3. John Berlau claims that the money-laundering tools expanded by the Patriot Act had never been effective and instead swamped agencies with useless information. Thus, he argues, expanding these tools to obtain even more information will not prove useful in combating terrorism. However, the Justice Department contends that these expanded tools have in fact reduced terrorist financing. Does Berlau's viewpoint suggest another possible explanation for the Justice Department's post–Patriot Act success at reducing terrorist financing other than the money-laundering tools expanded by the Patriot Act? Explain, citing from his viewpoint.

Chapter 2

1. Both Jim Cornehls and Ramesh Ponnuru agree that the Patriot Act is an expansion of law enforcement power. Cornehls believes this expansion is designed to spy on innocent American citizens while Ponnuru argues that the law was expanded to stop terrorists. Both cite evidence to support their arguments. Citing from the viewpoints, which evidence do you find most convincing?

2. Bernie Sanders, a congressional representative, believes that the Patriot Act is a threat to the privacy of library patrons. Robert S. Mueller, director of the Federal Bureau of Investigation, contends that the Patriot Act protects library patron privacy. How is each author's role in the U.S. government reflected in his argument? Explain, citing from each viewpoint.

3. Steven A. Osher does not trust law enforcement to effectively separate Internet addresses from Internet content and thus opposes applying telephone surveillance law to the Internet. Orin S. Kerr believes such fears are unfounded. What assumption about law enforcement underlies Kerr's argument? Is the validity of this assumption necessary to support his argument? Citing from the text, explain.

4. Some commentators contend that critics of the Patriot Act base their arguments on potential, rather than actual civil liberties violations. Of the authors in this chapter who oppose the Patriot Act, do any offer concrete evidence that the Patriot Act is violating civil liberties? Is it necessary that critics do so to be persuasive? Citing examples from the texts, explain your conclusion.

Chapter 3

1. The authors in this chapter who believe the Patriot Act should be terminated, amended, or repealed cite several different sections of the act and express different concerns about the act. Which sections and concerns about the Patriot Act are cited most often? Do you agree that these sections should be terminated, amended, or repealed? Explain your answer, providing evidence from the viewpoints in this chapter.

2. The authors who support the Patriot Act often claim that terrorism is a serious threat to national security. On the other hand, many of the authors who want to amend or repeal the Patriot Act refer to times in U.S. history during which civil liberties have been unnecessarily violated due to national security concerns. How is the terrorist threat today different from threats in the past? How is it the same? How does your assessment of the threat influence your reading of the viewpoints?

Chapter 4

1. In his speech on the Senate floor on October 25, 2001, Senator Russell Feingold made many of the same arguments made by the authors in this anthology who oppose the Patriot Act. Why do you think his concerns were ignored at the time?

2. Some analysts claim that the Justice Department released its report on Patriot Act successes in response to the growing opposition to the act. Do you think the report would induce the American Library Association or the National League of Cities to revoke their resolutions? What in each organization's viewpoint leads you to your conclusion?

Organizations to Contact

The editors have compiled the following list of organizations concerned with the issues debated in this book. The descriptions are derived from materials provided by the organizations. All have publications or information available for interested readers. The list was compiled on the date of publication of the present volume; the information provided here may change. Be aware that many organizations take several weeks or longer to respond to inquiries, so allow as much time as possible.

American Civil Liberties Union (ACLU)
125 Broad St., 18th Fl., New York, NY 10004-2400
(212) 549-2500
e-mail: aclu@aclu.org • Web site: www.aclu.org

The American Civil Liberties Union is a national organization that works to defend Americans' civil rights guaranteed by the U.S. Constitution, arguing that measures to protect national security should not compromise fundamental civil liberties. It publishes and distributes policy statements, pamphlets, and press releases with titles such as "Bigger Monster, Weaker Chains: The Growth of an American Surveillance Society" and "Seeking Truth from Justice: PATRIOT Propaganda—The Justice Department's Campaign to Mislead the Public About the USA PATRIOT Act," which are available on its Web site.

American Enterprise Institute
1150 Seventeenth St. NW, Washington, DC 20036
(202) 862-5800 • fax: (202) 862-7177
Web site: www.aei.org

The American Enterprise Institute for Public Policy Research is a scholarly research institute that is dedicated to preserving limited government, private enterprise, and a strong foreign policy and national defense. Articles about the Patriot Act, including "The Patriot Act Under Fire," can be found in its magazine, *American Enterprise*, and on its Web site.

The Brookings Institution
1775 Massachusetts Ave. NW, Washington, DC 20036
(202) 797-6000 • fax: (202) 797-6004
e-mail: brookinfo@brook.edu • Web site: www.brookings.org

The institution, founded in 1927, is a think tank that conducts research and education in foreign policy, economics, government, and the social sciences. Publications include the quarterly *Brook-

ings Review, periodic *Policy Briefs*, and books including *Protecting the American Homeland*. Articles, commentary, and speeches on the Patriot Act, including "Rights, Liberties, and Security: Recalibrating the Balance After September 11" and "The Rule of Law and Terrorism: The Critical Implications of a New National Debate," can be accessed using the Web site's search engine.

Cato Institute
1000 Massachusetts Ave. NW, Washington, DC 20001-5403
(202) 842-0200 • fax: (202) 842-3490
e-mail: cato@cato.org • Web site: www.cato.org

The institute is a nonpartisan public policy research foundation dedicated to limiting the role of government and protecting individual liberties. It publishes the quarterly magazine *Regulation*, the bimonthly *Cato Policy Report*, and numerous policy papers and articles. Articles on the Patriot Act include "More Surveillance Equals Less Liberty: Patriot Act Reduces Privacy, Undercuts Judicial Review," which is available on its Web site.

Center for Constitutional Rights (CCR)
666 Broadway, 7th Fl., New York, NY 10012
(212) 614-6464 • fax: (212) 614-6499
e-mail: info@ccr-ny.org • Web site: www.ccr-ny.org

The center is dedicated to the proposition that the dignity and physical integrity of all human beings is inviolable. CCR monitors government misconduct, holds corporations accountable, and fights for international human rights and for racial, social, and economic justice. The center uses litigation proactively to advance its mission. Articles on the Patriot Act are available on its Web site.

Center for Immigration Studies
1522 K St. NW, Suite 820, Washington, DC 20005-1202
(202) 466-8185 • fax: (202) 466-8076
e-mail: center@cis.org • Web site: www.cis.org

The Center for Immigration Studies is the nation's only think tank dedicated to research and analysis of the economic, social, and demographic impacts of immigration on the United States. An independent, nonpartisan, nonprofit research organization founded in 1985, the center aims to expand public support for an immigration policy that is both pro-immigrant and low-immigration. Among its publications are the backgrounders "The USA PATRIOT Act of 2001: A Summary of the Anti-Terrorism Law's Immigration-Related Provisions," which is available on its Web site.

Central Intelligence Agency (CIA)
Office of Public Affairs, Washington, DC 20505
(703) 482-0623 • fax: (703) 482-1739
Web site: www.cia.gov

President Harry S. Truman created the CIA in 1947 with the signing of the National Security Act (NSA). The NSA charged the Director of Central Intelligence (DCI) with coordinating the nation's intelligence activities and correlating, evaluating, and disseminating intelligence that affects national security. The CIA is an independent agency, responsible to the president through the DCI, and accountable to the American people through the Intelligence Oversight Committee of the U.S. Congress. Publications, including *Factbook on Intelligence*, are available on its Web site.

Council on American-Muslim Relations (CAIR)
453 New Jersey Ave. SE, Washington, DC 20003
(202) 488-8787 • fax: (202) 488-0833
e-mail: cair@cair-net.org • Web site: www.cair-net.org

CAIR is a nonprofit organization that challenges stereotypes of Islam and Muslims and offers an Islamic perspective on public policy issues. Its publications include action alerts, news briefs, and the quarterly newsletter *Faith in Action*. The CAIR Web site features statements condemning both the September 11, 2001, terrorist attacks and subsequent discrimination against Muslims.

Electronic Frontier Foundation (EFF)
454 Shotwell St., San Francisco, CA 94110
(415) 436-9333 • fax: (415) 436-9993
e-mail: eff@eff.org • Web site: www.eff.org

EFF is a watchdog organization for the preservation of civil liberties on the Internet. It develops positions on free speech, encryption, privacy, and intellectual property, and lobbies for them, providing guidance to the government and courts and supporting new technologies that preserve American freedoms. On its Web site, EFF provides links to articles and reports, including "EFF Analysis of the Provisions of the USA PATRIOT Act That Relate to Online Activities."

Electronic Privacy Information Center (EPIC)
1718 Connecticut Ave. NW, Suite 200, Washington, DC 20009
(202) 483-1140 • fax: (202) 483-1248
Web site: http://epic.org

EPIC is a public interest research center in Washington, DC. It was established in 1994 to focus public attention on emerging civil liberties issues and to protect privacy, the First Amendment, and constitutional values. EPIC publishes an e-mail and online newsletter on civil liberties in the information age, the *Epic Alert*. EPIC also publishes reports and books about privacy, open government, free speech, and other topics related to civil liberties. Articles, reports, testimony, and analysis on the Patriot Act are available using the EPIC Web site's search engine.

Federal Bureau of Investigation (FBI)

935 Pennsylvania Ave. NW, Room 7972, Washington, DC 20535
(202) 324-3000
Web site: www.fbi.gov

The FBI, the principal investigative arm of the U.S. Department of Justice, evolved from an unnamed force of Special Agents formed on July 26, 1909. It has the authority and responsibility to investigate specific crimes assigned to it. The FBI also is authorized to provide other law enforcement agencies with cooperative services, such as fingerprint identification, laboratory examinations, and police training. The mission of the FBI is to uphold the law through the investigation of violations of federal criminal law; to protect the United States from foreign intelligence and terrorist activities; to provide leadership and law enforcement assistance to federal, state, local, and international agencies; and to perform these responsibilities in a manner that is responsive to the needs of the public and is faithful to the Constitution of the United States. Press releases, congressional statements, and major speeches on issues concerning the FBI are available on the agency's Web site.

United States Department of Justice (DOJ)

950 Pennsylvania Ave. NW, Washington, DC 20530-0001
(202) 514-2000
e-mail: AskDOJ@usdoj.gov • Web site: www.usdoj.gov

The function of the DOJ is to enforce the law and defend the interests of the United States according to the law; to ensure public safety against foreign and domestic threats; to provide federal leadership in preventing and controlling crime; to seek just punishment for those guilty of unlawful behavior; to administer and enforce the nation's immigration laws fairly and effectively; and to ensure fair and impartial administration of justice for all Americans. On its Web site, the DOJ provides a link to its Web site, Preserving Life & Liberty, launched to educate Americans about how the department is preserving life and liberty by using the Patriot Act. Also published on its Web site is "Report from the Field: The USA PATRIOT Act at Work."

Bibliography of Books

Kurt M. Campbell and Michele A. Flourney
To Prevail: An American Strategy for the Campaign Against Terrorism. Washington, DC: Center for Strategic and International Studies, 2001.

Nancy Chang et al.
Silencing Political Dissent: How Post–September 11 Anti-Terrorism Measures Threaten Our Civil Liberties. New York: Seven Stories Press, 2002.

David Cole
Enemy Aliens: Double Standards and Constitutional Freedoms in the War on Terrorism. New York: New Press, 2003.

David Cole and James X. Dempsey
Terrorism and the Constitution: Sacrificing Civil Liberties in the Name of National Security. New York: New Press, 2002.

Lynn E. Davis
Organizing for Homeland Security. Santa Monica, CA: Rand, 2002.

Alan M. Dershowitz
Shouting Fire: Civil Liberties in a Turbulent Age. Boston: Little, Brown, 2002.

Steven Emerson
American Jihad: The Terrorist Living Among Us. New York: Free Press, 2002.

Herbert N. Foerstel
Refuge of a Scoundrel: The Patriot Act in Libraries. Westport, CT: Libraries Unlimited, 2004.

Tedd Gottfried
Homeland Security vs. Constitutional Rights. Brookfield, CT: Twenty-First Century Books, 2003.

Katrina Vanden Heuvel, ed.
A Just Response: The Nation *on Terrorism, Democracy, and September 11, 2001.* New York: Thunder's Mouth Press, 2002.

Philip B. Heymann
Terrorism and America: A Commonsense Strategy for a Democratic Society. Cambridge, MA: MIT Press, 1998.

Misha Klein and Adrian McIntyre, eds.
September 11, Contests and Consequences: An Anthology. Berkeley, CA: Copy Central, 2001.

Lawyers Committee for Human Rights
Assessing the New Normal: Liberty and Security for the Post–September 11 United States. New York: Lawyers Committee for Human Rights, 2003.

Lawyers Committee for Human Rights
Imbalance of Powers: How Changes to U.S. Law & Policy Since 9/11 Erode Human Rights and Civil Liberties. New York: Lawyers Committee for Human Rights, 2003.

Michael A. Ledeen
The War Against the Terror Masters. New York: St. Martin's Press, 2002.

Philip M. Melanson — *Secrecy Wars: National Security, Privacy, and the Public's Right to Know*. Washington, DC: Brassey's, 2001.

C. William Michaels — *No Greater Threat: America After September 11 and the Rise of a National Security State*. New York: Algora, 2002.

Donald J. Musch, ed. — *Civil Liberties and the Foreign Intelligence Surveillance Act*. Dobbs Ferry, NY: Oceana, 2003.

Michael E. O'Hanlon — *Protecting the American Homeland: A Preliminary Analysis*. Washington, DC: Brookings Institution, 2002.

William H. Rehnquist — *All the Laws but One: Civil Liberties in Wartime*. New York: Knopf, 1998.

Stephen J. Schulhofer — *The Enemy Within: Intelligence Gathering, Law Enforcement, and Civil Liberties in the Wake of September 11*. New York: Century Foundation Press, 2002.

Phil Scraton, ed. — *Beyond September 11: An Anthology of Dissent*. London: Pluto Press, 2002.

Jeffrey D. Simon — *The Terrorist Trap: America's Experience with Terrorism*. Bloomington: Indiana University Press, 2001.

Peter S. Watson — *The Economic Arsenal in the War Against Terrorism*. Washington, DC: National Legal Center for the Public Interest, 2002.

William H. Webster — *"No Time to Be Wobbly": Protecting Our Homeland, Preserving Our Values*. Washington, DC: National Legal Center for the Public Interest, 2003.

Paul Wilkinson — *Terrorism Versus Democracy: The Liberal State Response*. London: Frank Cass, 2001.

Index